THE

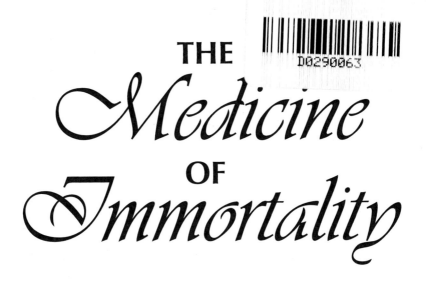

Medicine

OF

Immortality

An ABC Approach to
Eucharistic Meditation

Msgr. Joseph Diermeier

New Hope Publications

IMPRIMATUR:
+ Most Rev. William Patrick Callahan
Bishop of La Crosse
January 25, 2021

Declaration

For additional copies of this book, contact:
New Hope Publications
PO Box 10
New Hope, KY 40052
270-325-3061
www.newhope-ky.org

Ask for stock #3470.
Text ©2021 Msgr. Joseph Diermeier
ISBN 978-1-892875-87-7

Table of Contents

The author and publisher wish to thank St. Francis de Sales Parish in Ajax, Ontario, Canada for providing the photo of the beautiful pelican symbol seen on the front cover of this book. The image adorns their adoration chapel's altar. The original artwork was done by Mario Cassar of Malta in Europe.

From the parish's website:

The symbol of the mother pelican feeding her little baby pelicans is rooted in ancient legend which precedes Christianity. The legend was that in time of famine, the mother pelican would wound herself, striking her breast with her beak in order to feed her young with her own blood to prevent starvation.

For Catholics the pelican symbolizes Jesus our Redeemer, who gave His life for our redemption and made atonement for our sins through His passion and death. We were dead in sin and have found new life through the Blood of Christ. Moreover, Jesus continues to feed us with His Body and Blood in the Holy Eucharist.

Introduction

May my meditation be pleasing to Him;
I will rejoice in the Lord.
(Ps 104:34)

I remember reading about a fatal air disaster that occurred in 1987. A plane crashed shortly after takeoff at a Michigan airport, resulting in the deaths of 156 people. Among those who died were a father and mother and their six-year-old son. Their four-year-old daughter was the sole survivor in the crash. Some said that the reason the little girl lived was because her mother had shielded the girl with her own body. In a sense, it can be said that the mother gave her body to protect the life of the little child who was able to live on because of her mother's love.

Two thousand years ago Jesus shielded us with His body. He gave His body, His life, to save us from a terrible disaster— not an air disaster, but one whereby sin could have claimed our lives. He gave His body to protect us, and we are able to live on because of His love. On the night before He died, Jesus gave the very same instruction to His apostles. He told them, "Remain in my love" (Jn 15:9). In these words Jesus was preparing His apostles for their first Eucharist. They were going to receive His body and blood. The words that Jesus spoke at the Last Supper were not simply for the apostles; they are for us as well. Remaining in Christ's love is our vocation. We are called to live on in the love of Jesus. When Jesus pronounced those words, He hoped that His presence would remain with the apostles as they continued to live as He had taught them. Through their ongoing words and actions, even after His death and rising, the apostles were to re-present and re-enact Christ's love.

The love of Jesus is a very special kind of love. He loved through His teaching, through His compassion, forgiving sinners and healing the sick. In the Eucharist Jesus gave us the greatest way for His compassion, forgiveness and healing to occur. He gave us what Saint Ignatius of Antioch called the "medicine of immortality." Father John Horn, S.J., echoes the same sentiment about Jesus' healing in these words: "The key to participating in Christ's deepest healing graces resides in one's willingness and ability to rest safely in prayer, contemplating, as a child, God's loving gaze."[1] That's what this little book is about—"participating in Christ's deepest healing graces." We are invited to experience these graces in the Eucharist.

The reflections that follow are an attempt to experience Christ as "the companion whom we can see only in the shadows, but whose reality fills our whole life and makes us yearn to be with Him forever."[2] These reflections are, in the words of Pope Emeritus Benedict XVI, about "the center of Christian life and the very existence of the Church." In a written statement following the 2019 Vatican summit with regard to clergy sexual abuse, the Pope Emeritus offered the following:

> The Second Vatican Council was rightly focused on returning this sacrament of the Presence of His Person, of His Passion, Death and Resurrection, to the center of Christian life and the very existence of the Church. In part, this really has come about, and we should be most grateful to the Lord for it.

> And yet a rather different attitude is prevalent. What predominates is not a new reverence for the presence of Christ's death and resurrection, but a way of dealing with Him that destroys the greatness of the Mystery. The declining participation in the Sunday Eucharistic celebration shows how little we Christians of today still know about appreciating the greatness of the gift that consists in His Real Presence.

1   John Horn, S.J., *Healing Prayer: Practical Mysticism and St. Ignatius' Spiritual Exercises* (Institute of Priestly Formation, 2013).
2   Saint Josémaria Escriva, *Christ Is Passing By* (New York: Scepter, 1974), n. 116.

The Eucharist is devalued into a mere ceremonial gesture when it is taken for granted that courtesy requires Him to be offered at family celebrations or on occasions such as weddings and funerals to all those invited for family reasons.

The way people often simply receive the Holy Sacrament in communion as a matter of course shows that many see communion as a purely ceremonial gesture. Therefore, when thinking about what action is required first and foremost, it is rather obvious that we do not need another Church of our own design. Rather, what is required first and foremost is the renewal of the Faith in the Reality of Jesus Christ given to us in the Blessed Sacrament.[3]

I have written these reflections with one goal in mind: I hope that they remind us that Eucharistic meditation allows us to have an intimate conversation with God Himself. There is a humorous story that illustrates a conversation with God. As the story goes, Mr. Smith decided that he needed to go on a diet, so he changed his route so as to avoid a bakery where he would stop to buy a few sweets every morning as he drove to work. He took the alternate route for several days, but then one morning he inadvertently drove past the bakery. There they were—brownies, doughnuts, cheesecakes and sweet rolls in the display window. He thought that perhaps this was no accident and that God had intended this to happen. So he prayed: "Lord, I leave this up to you. If you want me to stop in and purchase some baked goods, then please see to it that a parking space is available right in front of the bakery." Sure enough, a place opened up—on his eighth time around the block!

On a more serious note, I am writing these reflections as a way to describe the prayer that I use after receiving Holy Communion. It is a short prayer that helps me to appreciate, as Pope Benedict XVI put it, "the greatness of the Mystery." The "Mystery" is that Christ is not relegated to past history; He is really present today. Because of that, we not only *speak about Jesus* and His Real Presence in the Eucharist; we

---

3   Pope Emeritus Benedict XVI, essay published on April 10, 2019.

also have the opportunity to *speak to Jesus* who is really present in the Blessed Sacrament. Jesus is really present as the living God who became man at His Incarnation. His presence in the Blessed Sacrament continues His Incarnation among us until the end of time. The prayer that I offer after receiving Holy Communion helps me to appreciate how Christ has come to me and to so many others in a personal and intimate way. When Jesus is received in Holy Communion, He has humbly assumed the appearances of bread and wine, desiring in this veiled way to be bodily connected to us.

We receive the divine life of God in the sacraments. To recognize that we receive divine life is essential for our understanding of what sacraments are and what they offer. In the Eucharist we are privileged to receive, under the appearances of bread and wine, Jesus who is *completely* present in His body, blood, soul and divinity. In the host and in the wine that are consecrated during the Mass, Christ is present entirely in each of these elements. The tiniest fraction of a consecrated Host or the merest drop of consecrated wine contains the entirety of Jesus' real and sacramental presence. Whether we receive under one element or both, we are receiving the *whole* Jesus into our bodies in order to nourish our souls.

When Jesus died on the Cross, some thought it was a fitting punishment for a criminal who had committed blasphemy. Others, including ourselves, believe that Christ offered Himself in atonement for the sins of all. In that event of His suffering and death, Jesus healed the severed relationship that humankind had with God the Father. Jesus took on sin in order to take away sin. Saint Paul states in his letter to the Galatians (see 3:7-14) that Christ took on the "curse" that was mentioned in the Book of Deuteronomy (see 21:23) in order to take away the curse (see 27:26) that we were under because of sin. Further, on the night before His death and while giving thanks during the Passover meal, Jesus was offering to His disciples the pledge of His love. The sacrament of the Eucharist prolongs these events and actualizes them. In the sacrament of the Eucharist God comes to meet us. He receives us with His love, and we receive Him with our love. That's the beauty of the sacrament.

The opportunity for us to give thanks for the sacrament which offers the divine presence of Christ in Holy Communion is mentioned in *The General Instruction of the Roman Missal*. It states the following: "When the distribution of Communion is over, if appropriate, the priest and faithful pray quietly for some time."[4] The *General Instruction* also states that after Holy Communion has been distributed, a "sacred silence may be observed for some time."[5]

Another source that reminds us of the importance of silent prayer and thanksgiving after receiving Our Lord in Holy Communion is the document called *The Year of the Eucharist: Suggestions and Proposals*. This document was issued in 2004 by the Congregation for the Divine Worship and the Discipline of the Sacraments. In the document we find the following:

> Silence is a necessary element for recollection, interiorization, and inner prayer within the rhythm of the liturgical celebration. It is not mere emptiness or absence, but rather presence, receptiveness, responsiveness to the God who both speaks to and works for us, here and now. "Remain in silence before the Lord," Psalm 37:7 reminds us.
>
> The truth is that prayer with its different aspects—praise, petition, invocation, exclamation, lamentation, thanksgiving—is built upon the foundation of silence.
>
> Two moments of particular significance within the Eucharistic celebration are the silence after the readings of the Word of God and above all, after Communion with the Body and Blood of the Lord. These moments of silence are prolonged, in a certain sense, even outside the liturgical celebration in prayerful visits—in adoration and contemplation—to the Blessed Sacrament.[6]

---

4   *The Roman Missal,* 2011. "The Structure of the Mass, Its Elements and Its Parts," 88.

5   Ibid., "The Different Forms of Celebrating Mass," 164.

6   Congregation for Divine Worship and the Discipline of the Sacraments, *The Year of the Eucharist: Suggestions and Proposals*, n. 28.

Pope Francis has given us an apostolic exhortation, *Gaudete et Exsultate*, on the call to holiness in today's world. What I especially like about this document is that Pope Francis quotes a number of saints with regard to various practices by which we can grow in holiness—one of them being the practice of silence. For example, he writes:

> Saint John of the Cross tells us: "Endeavor to remain always in the presence of God, whether it is real, imaginative, or unitive, insofar as is permitted by your works." In the end, our desire for God will surely find expression in our daily lives: "Try to be continuous in prayer, and in the midst of bodily exercises to not leave it. Whether you eat, drink, talk with others, or do anything, always go to God and attach your heart to him."[7]

Pope Francis then offered specific and practical methods for interior silence to occur.

> For this to happen, however, some moments spent alone with God are also necessary. For Saint Teresa of Avila, prayer "is nothing but friendly intercourse, and frequent solitary conversation with him who we know loves us." I would insist that this is true not only for a privileged few, but for all of us, for "we all have need of this silence, filled with the presence of him who is adored." Trust-filled prayer is a response of a heart open to encountering God face to face, where all is peaceful and the quiet voice of the Lord can be heard in the midst of silence.[8]

The approach that I take for the prayer after Communion amounts to recalling certain words or phrases that use the first three letters of the alphabet: A, B and C. For example, using the letter "A" provides the following words for the prayer: *amazement, astonishment, awareness* and *attitude*. As I begin

---

7 Pope Francis, Apostolic Exhortation *Gaudete et Exsultate*, March 19, 2018, 148. Here the Holy Father cites from Saint John of the Cross in *Degrees of Perfection*, 2 and *Counsels to a Religious on How to Attain Perfection*, 9.
8 Ibid, 149. In this paragraph Pope Francis cites the *Autobiography* of Saint Teresa of Avila as well as the 1995 Apostolic Letter *Orientale Lumen* of Pope John Paul II.

the prayer I try to recall the kind of *amazement* that I should have, and actually do have, for the way that God revealed His love by sending His Son, Jesus, among us. It is amazing to think that God, whose angel drove the first sinners from the Garden of Eden, would want to rescue humankind from its sinful condition by becoming like us in all things but sin. I then recall the level of *astonishment* that I should have in realizing that Jesus, although ascended into heaven, continues to remain with us in the simplicity of bread and wine that become His body and blood. The prayer then proceeds to my *awareness* of the body and blood of Christ within me and how I am invited to live this day with the *attitude* of Jesus Christ. The "A" words are then followed by words or phrases that are associated with the letter "B" and subsequently by those that begin with the letter "C." The prayer and brief reflection take about two minutes. Later in the day when time permits, I use that prayer in a period of meditation.

In the reflection that follows, each of the A-B-C words or phrases will have a similar format:

    a) a passage from Scripture to highlight the word or phrase;

    b) a reflection within a scriptural or spiritual context;

    c) an example to assist with a deeper understanding of the word or phrase being considered; and

    d) a brief summary statement followed by a concluding thought pertaining to the word or phrase being examined that comes from one of the early Church Fathers, from a papal encyclical or from another prominent source that provides spiritual enrichment.

This meditation has helped me to appreciate more fully the gift of the Eucharist and my relationship with Jesus—or perhaps even better stated, Jesus' relationship with me. In Chapter 17 of John's Gospel we find the prayer of Jesus on the night of the Last Supper. Referring to His followers, Jesus said: "I pray for them" (17:9)—and then again,

> I pray not only for them, but also for those who will believe in me through their word, so that they may all be one, as you, Father, are in me and I in you, that they also may be in us, that the world may believe that you sent me" (17:20-21).

This is what Jesus continues to do for us. He prays for us in heaven and He prays for us in His Eucharistic presence throughout the world. That is part of the great "Mystery." Jesus has risen from death and has ascended to heaven. He is glorified. Nevertheless, the living and glorified Christ is really present in the Eucharist. It is the glorified Lord Jesus who intercedes for us in heaven but is also really present with us in the sacrament of the Holy Eucharist.

The Second Vatican Council's *Decree on the Ministry and Life of Priests (Presbyterorum ordinis)* contains the following thoughts about the Eucharist in paragraph 5 of the document:

> For the most holy Eucharist holds within itself the whole spiritual treasure of the Church, namely Christ himself, our Passover and our living bread, who through His flesh, now made alive and life-giving by the Spirit, offers life to human beings, who are in turn invited and drawn to offer themselves, their labors and all creation in union with Him.[9]

If these reflections can be of help to you, then God be praised. My hope is that whoever reads these reflections not only thinks about the Real Presence of Christ in the Blessed Sacrament but also realizes that we can speak to Him, for He is really present. We can speak to Christ who is present in the Eucharist and we can tell Him about our joys, sorrows, hurts, disappointments, goals, dreams, desires, needs, and so on. A recent Pew Research Center study reported that 69% of U.S. Catholics believe that the bread and wine at Mass remain only "symbols" of the Body and Blood of Jesus, even after

---

9   Second Vatican Council, *Decree on the Ministry and Life of Priests (Presbyterorum ordinis)*, Dec. 7, 1965.

consecration.[10] This statistic is what has motivated me to offer these reflections. May our Blessed Mother and other saintly allies, especially those who were so devoted to the Eucharist, guide us so that we might hope to adore Jesus in a manner that is most fitting for His Eucharistic entry into our lives and into the world that so badly needs Him.

Meditate, as you should, upon what you eat, what you drink, to what you answer "Amen."

(St. Augustine)

---

10   This statistic is provided by the Pew Research Center in a study conducted from February 4-19, 2019.

My Communion Meditation Prayer

The entire prayer that I use for the Communion meditation, and on which this book's reflections are based, is as follows:

*Jesus, although You have existed with the Father and the Holy Spirit from the beginning, You came among us in your human nature and showed us the depth of divine love. With **amazement** I think about how You, Almighty God, became man. Even more, with **astonishment** I recall Your words to Your disciples that to have eternal life, we have to eat the bread that is You. Jesus, I have now received the miracle of Your flesh and blood in this Holy Communion. May I grow in the **awareness** that Your divine life is now within me. Please let my **attitude** reflect Your presence in me.*

*Lord Jesus, **I believe** that You are truly present within the consecrated **bread** which has been **blessed and broken**. Through the eyes of faith I affirm that what I have received is Your **Body and Blood**.*

*Lord Jesus, in this **celebration of faith** I have received the **cup of blessing**. It is the new and eternal **covenant** of Your love. May I proclaim once again this day that You are the **Christ**, the Anointed One of God, who has come to me. Amen.*

A

This is the first part of my Communion meditation:

*Jesus, although You have existed with the Father and the Holy Spirit from the beginning, You came among us in Your human nature and showed us the depth of divine love. With **amazement** I think about how You, Almighty God, became man. Even more, with **astonishment** I recall Your words to Your disciples, that to have eternal life we have to eat the bread that is You. Jesus, I have now received the miracle of Your flesh and blood in this Holy Communion. May I grow in the **awareness** that Your divine life is now within me. Please let my **attitude** reflect Your presence in me.*

****

Amazement – Astonishment – Awareness – Attitude

****

Amazement

The Father loves his son and shows him everything that he himself does, and he will show him greater works than these, so that you may be **amazed**.

(Jn 5:20)

There are certain things that most of us would say are amazing. On a clear night when I look at the stars, I am amazed to think that beyond the stars that are seen, there are billions more that exist. Beyond the portion of the Milky Way galaxy that can be seen, there are other planets and systems even beyond our solar system. We can be amazed and stand in awe. When I say that I am amazed by something, I mean that even though I believe it, I remain in awe. In this example, amazement occurs as an expression of something 1) marvelous or 2) seemingly unbelievable.

To be amazed at the goodness of God requires the virtue of faith. Unless one has the gift of faith, it is impossible to speak about the goodness of God. For example, without the gift of faith, the goodness of God offered to us in the Eucharist makes no sense. Without the gift of faith there can be no real understanding or appreciation that in the Eucharist Christ is sacramentally present in His body, blood, soul and divinity. Without the gift of faith, there can be no real understanding of what God has done and continues to do for us. In that line of thought Peter Kreeft, a well-respected philosopher and theologian, writes the following:

> Why in the world God, the perfect Being who has no needs whatever, wants to be not only in relationship with but friends with the likes of us stupid, silly, shallow, sinful

creatures surpasses all human knowing; but that is the Good
News of the world's most popular and beloved Book.[1]

It is only with the gift of faith that we can believe that
God has called us to be His children and heirs to the promise made to us through Jesus. It is only with the gift of faith
that we can acknowledge the presence of Jesus in His glorified human body seated at the right hand of the Father in
heaven—and also in every tabernacle here on earth. It is only
with the gift of faith that we can believe in the real presence
of Jesus in His glorified body in heaven—and here on earth
in the Holy Eucharist.

For us to believe in the words that are contained in the
Sacred Scriptures, the gift of faith is essential. In the following
reflections, I can only appeal to those who have faith in the
power and the beauty of God's goodness as it is offered to us
in the Eucharist. Anyone who possesses the gift of faith in the
Eucharist will find that the rewards are immense.

In the Gospel according to John, we read that "God so
loved the world that he gave his only Son, so that everyone
who believes in him might not perish but might have eternal
life" (3:16). What emotion would be more appropriate on our
part than sheer amazement in realizing that God loved us so
much that He sent His Son into our world and into our lives?
That is why I begin the meditation after receiving Holy Communion by realizing that I am (and truly need to be) amazed
that God came to us—to me—with love and merciful compassion when He sent His Son into this world. The *Catechism of
the Catholic Church* states the following:

> The Eucharist, the sacrament of our salvation accomplished
> by Christ on the cross, is also a sacrifice of praise in thanks-
> giving for the work of creation. In the Eucharistic sacri-
> fice the whole of creation loved by God is presented to the
> Father through the death and the Resurrection of Christ.
> Through Christ the Church can offer the sacrifice of praise

1   Peter Kreeft, *Doors in the Walls of the World: Signs of Transcendence in the Human Story* (Ignatius Press, San Francisco, 2018), 61.

in thanksgiving for all God has made good, beautiful, and just in creation and in humanity.[2]

A beautiful passage from the Letter to the Hebrews reveals to us that God was with us and spoke to us in a variety of ways. We read the following:

> In times past, God spoke in partial and various ways to our ancestors through the prophets; in these last days, he spoke to us through a son, whom he made heir of all things and through whom he created the universe (1:1).

When the author of the Letter to the Hebrews writes about "these last days," he is proclaiming by means of a parallel path the same message that Saint Paul preached and which we find in his Letter to the Galatians (4:4) where Paul spoke about how in the "fullness of time" God sent His Son among us.

In the letter of Saint Paul we read the following: "But when the fullness of time had come, God sent his son, born of a woman, born under the law, to ransom those under the law, so that we might receive adoption" (Gal 4:4). A little earlier in the letter, Saint Paul noted that God's justification of the Gentiles was based on the promise that God had made to bless all the nations through Abraham (see Gn 18:18). Developing this line of thought, Paul declared that "the blessing of Abraham might be extended to the Gentiles through Christ Jesus, so that we might receive the promise of the Spirit through faith" (Gal 3:14). From these Scripture passages we are taught about how in the fullness of time Jesus came among us. Jesus, born into a Jewish heritage, has also come to offer the Spirit to everyone, Jew and Gentile. Jesus, who lived two thousand years ago when He walked this earth, still lives in His risen and glorified humanity. He promised to remain with us until the end of time. In Christ's body and blood, He remains with us and He continues to nourish us with His Spirit.

---

2 *Catechism of the Catholic Church*, second edition (Washington, D.C.: United States Conference of Catholic Bishops, 1997), n. 1359.

While the Scriptures reveal the continuing presence of Jesus in the Eucharist, one of the earliest references about the Eucharist not contained in the Scriptures comes from Saint Ignatius of Antioch, who died in 107 A.D. As he was being led to Rome to suffer martyrdom, the bishop of Antioch wrote several letters which indicate the amazement that he felt as he experienced the Eucharistic mystery. With the use of some beautiful allusions, Ignatius wrote the following:

> I am God's grain, and I am being ground by the teeth of wild beasts in order that I may be pure bread for Christ... There is within me ... living water, speaking in me and saying within me, "Come to the Father." I take no pleasure in corruptible food or in the delights of this life. I want the Bread of God, which is the Flesh of Jesus Christ, who is of the seed of David; and as drink I want His Blood, which is incorruptible love.[3]

Saint Ignatius of Antioch knew that the Eucharist was the "source and summit" of the early ecclesial life of the Church, a phrase that would be used almost two thousand years later in the document *Lumen Gentium* from the Second Vatican Ecumenical Council.[4]

****

October 12, 2008 is a date that will remain in the minds and hearts of Catholics in Sokolka, Poland. During the morning Mass a consecrated Host fell to the floor during the distribution of Holy Communion. In accord with liturgical norms the Host was placed in a small vessel of water where it was expected that it would dissolve and then be disposed of properly. A week later the vessel with the Host was examined. Although the Host remained largely intact, there appeared a red stain like blood on it. The pastor, not knowing the cause for the altered appearance of the Host, notified his bishop. The bishop, in turn, examined

---

3 Francis X. Funk, *Patres Apostolici* (Tubingen, Germany, 1901), 130.
4 Vatican Council II, Dogmatic Constitution *Lumen gentium*, "On the Church," n. 11. English translation by Norman Tanner, S.J., ed., *Decrees of the Ecumenical Councils* (Sheed and Ward: London, 1990), 857.

it and determined that the Sacred Host should be removed from the water and placed on a small corporal. It was then preserved in the parish tabernacle. Subsequently the bishop determined that histopathological studies should be done on the Host.

A portion of the Host was analyzed by two medical experts who conducted independent studies in January of 2009. Both studies were described in detail and also photographed. The results from both studies concurred, stating that the fragment of the Host which had been examined was identical to the myocardial tissue of a person who is nearing death. A statement from the archbishop's office stated the following:

> The Sokolka event is not opposed to the faith of the Church; rather, it confirms it. The Church professes that, after the words of consecration, by the power of the Holy Spirit the bread is transformed into the Body of Christ, and the wine into His Blood. Additionally, this is an invitation for all ministers of the Eucharist to distribute the Body of the Lord with faith and care, and for the faithful to receive Him with adoration.

Some might think of this as an isolated incident. However, a similar incident occurred in 1996 in Buenos Aires when the future Pope Francis was an auxiliary bishop of the archdiocese. On August 18 of that year, while Father Alejandro Pezet was celebrating the Holy Mass, a woman told him that a discarded Host was in the back of the church. Father Pezet recovered the Host and placed it in a container of water that he set in the tabernacle. Two days later the priest noticed that the Host appeared bloody. He informed the bishop. The decision was made eventually to have the Host scientifically analyzed. Doctor Frederic Zugibe, a cardiologist and forensic pathologist, submitted a statement indicating that the analyzed material was a piece of the heart muscle and that the heart had been under severe stress. At the time when he submitted his report, he did not yet know that what he had examined was a consecrated Host. After being informed of this, he commented that it was an inexplicable mystery.

****

Summary statement:

It is only with profound amazement at the world around us that we will ever begin to understand the depths of God's love, a love first expressed in creation of the human person made in God's image and likeness, and a love that has continued through His ongoing self-revelation. The Eucharist is the greatest mystery of God's continuing self-revelation of love. Saint John Paul II, in his 2004 Letter to Priests for Holy Thursday, wrote the following:

> Before this extraordinary reality we find ourselves amazed and overwhelmed, so deep is the humility by which God "stoops" in order to unite himself with man! If we feel moved before the crib, when we contemplate the Incarnation of the Word, what must we feel before the altar where, by the poor hands of the priest, Christ makes his Sacrifice present in time? We can only fall to our knees and silently adore this supreme mystery of faith.[5]

Because the Word says, "This is my Body," let us be attentive, let us believe and let us look upon him with the eyes of the spirit. For Christ did not give something sensible; even in the sensible things, all is spiritual ... How many there are who still say, "I want to see his shape, his image, his clothing, his sandals." Behold, you do see him, you touch him, you eat him! You want to see his clothing. He gives himself to you, not just to be seen and to be touched but to be eaten and to be received within ... Let all of you be ardent, fervent and enthusiastic. If the Jews stood, shoes on, staff in hand, and eating in haste, how much more vigilant should you be. They were about to go to Palestine; ... you are about to go to heaven.

St. John Chrysostom, *Homily 82 on the Gospel of Matthew*

---

5   John Paul II, *Letter of the Holy Father to Priests for Holy Thursday 2004*, n. 2.

Astonishment

Then **astonishment** seized them all and they glorified God,
and, struck with awe, they said,
"We have seen incredible things today."

(Lk 5:26)

Many people use the words *amazement* and *astonishment* interchangeably. I don't. I am amazed by a variety of persons, places and things, and I accept their existence as marvelous or as something almost unbelievable. By way of distinction, when I am astonished about something, it is because I was prepared for something else to occur.

An example may help. On October 16, 1978 the world received most surprising news: that a Polish Cardinal had been elected as Pope! The new Pope said that he had come "from a country far ... far away." This was so unexpected that it astonished many. Due to his intellectual skills, his engaging personality, and his deep union with God in prayer, Pope John Paul II accomplished much that many would also consider astonishing. From the day of his election to his recovery after an assassination attempt to his efforts to help lay the groundwork for freedom in Eastern Europe—these and many other unexpected events marked a pontificate that was an *astonishing* blessing for the Church and the world.

Astonishment is an emotion that takes hold of us when something other than what we had expected occurs. If we think about the life of Jesus, His miracles, and the stories He preached, and the way He outmaneuvered those who tried to entrap Him in speech, we might feel astonishment. Jesus often said and did things that were not expected. One of the first of those times is revealed in the Gospel according to Luke. We read that when Jesus was twelve years old, He accompanied His parents and relatives to Jerusalem for the feast of Passover. Heading homeward, Mary and Joseph realized that Jesus was not among the group in their caravan. They returned to Jerusalem and found Jesus in the Temple, "sitting in the midst of the teachers, listening to them and asking them questions, and all who heard him were astounded at his understanding and his answers" (Lk 2:46-47). One would not have expected a young adolescent to be as well-versed as Jesus was when He sat among the scholars and answered the questions that they posed. We could assume that they were somewhat astonished to hear a young lad answer questions of theological depth.

The Lucan passage tells us that in addition to the scholars being astounded by Jesus' understanding of Scripture, Mary and Joseph were also astonished, not because of the questions and answers that Jesus gave as He sat with the teachers, but because He remained behind in Jerusalem and did something they had not expected from Him. Mary even said to Jesus that she and Joseph had been searching for Him. She asked why He had done this—presumably questioning why He remained in Jerusalem without any indication that He was not going to join the caravan for the homeward trek. Jesus' response to her question is itself astonishing, for He said, "Did you not know that I must be in my Father's house?" "But they did not understand what what He said to them" (Lk 2:49-50). Jesus' reply to His parents indicated that He understood His identity as the Son of God. Further, if Mary and Joseph were astonished by the fact that Jesus deliberately remained in Jerusalem without telling them when they departed the city, they must have been all the more astonished when they heard Jesus refer to God as His Father and to the Temple as His Father's house.

Over the last few years a prominent biblical scholar, Dr. Brant Pitre, has made significant contributions to our understanding of the Eucharist. He reflects the change from amazement to astonishment when he examines what occurred during the Last Supper:

But at his final Passover, on the night of the Last Supper, Jesus did something strange. During that meal, instead of speaking about the past exodus from Egypt, Jesus talked about his future suffering and death. On that night, instead of explaining the meaning of the flesh of the Passover lamb, Jesus identified the bread and wine of the supper as his own body and blood, and commanded the disciples to eat and drink.[1]

Dr. Pitre's words help us move from the amazement of the Passover event and its story of God's protection and providence for His chosen people to the astonishment that was to occur in the event of the Last Supper and in the future event of Christ remaining with us under the form of bread and wine until He comes again in glory. You can imagine the astonishment of the apostles when they heard the words of Jesus who said, "This is my body" and "This is my blood" over the bread and wine. They had to be astonished because they could not possibly have imagined ahead of time what was to occur.

It is difficult *not* to be astonished with what occurs during the Eucharist. Every time the Holy Sacrifice of the Mass is celebrated validly, the miracle of bread and wine becoming the body and blood of Jesus Christ occurs. In this, the bread and wine cease being bread and wine, instead becoming the glorified body and blood of Our Lord. How can we not be astonished?

Similarly, how can we not be astonished when we consider how the early Church had to wrestle with heresies which denied either the divinity or the humanity of Jesus? One would ordinarily expect that with such diverse opinions among the early Christians that the Church would not have continued with the strength of conviction that it had. Of all the early heresies, perhaps the one most commonly known and certainly the one that had fueled intense controversy was that of Arianism. In the early 300s, a priest named Arius taught that Jesus was a

---

1   Brant Pitre, *Jesus and the Jewish Roots of the Eucharist: Unlocking the Secrets of the Last Supper* (Doubleday: New York, 2011), 49.

great human being, but that He was not God. The Council of Nicaea condemned this heresy in 325 A.D., stating that Jesus Christ is true God and true man. In proclaiming that Jesus is true God and true man, the Church was also stating that in order to redeem us, Jesus had to be both God and man. He took on human nature to make atonement for our sins; He was and is true God so that the atonement would have infinite value. All of this is astonishing.

What about the astonishment that we should have when we consider what occurs during the Mass when the bread and wine are consecrated? There are some who believe that the bread and wine are merely *symbols* of Christ's presence among us. This is incorrect because the bread and wine that become transformed during the Holy Mass truly do become the body and blood of Jesus. If His presence is *only* symbolic in the consecrated bread and wine, then we are committing a serious sin by worshiping these elements as though they were God Himself. Idolatry would be the only possible conclusion if Christ were only symbolically present in the Eucharist. However, we realize that Christ comes to us in a sacramental form—which means that Jesus is present among us under the appearances of bread and wine and not in His own proper form as when He walked the earth two thousand years ago. That, too, is astonishing.

Although the bread and wine are not merely symbols of Christ, there is something symbolic about them. For example, bread and wine give nourishment; so does the Eucharist. Another symbol that can be found exists in the realization that often good food in the form of bread (cookies, cakes, pies, etc.) and wine brings folks together. Similarly, when we celebrate the Holy Eucharist, the bread and wine are used to bring folks together for a very special purpose. A meal, therefore, can symbolize the unity among family members or friends.

Just as Dr. Pitre's words move us from amazement at God's presence in the world to the astonishment of how Christ continues to be in the world through the sacrament of Holy Communion, Saint John Paul II expressed a similar thought when he wrote:

> I would like to rekindle Eucharistic "amazement." … To contemplate Christ involves being able to recognize Him wherever He manifests himself, in His many forms of presence, but above all in the living sacrament of His body and His blood. *The Church draws her life from Christ in the Eucharist*; by Him she is fed and by Him she is enlightened. The Eucharist is both a mystery of faith and a mystery of light. Whenever the Church celebrates the Eucharist, the faithful can in some way relive the experience of the two disciples on the road to Emmaus: "Their eyes were opened and they recognized Him" (Lk 24:31).[2]

The two disciples on the road to Emmaus were astonished when their eyes were opened to recognize Jesus. Before that, however, "beginning with Moses and all the prophets, he interpreted to them what referred to him in all the scriptures" (Lk 24:27). They celebrated the Liturgy of the Word—followed by their first Communion. When Jesus offered the blessing over the bread, their eyes were opened. They were most probably looking intently at the bread—and that is when Jesus vanished. Now the question: Could Jesus have been teaching us that from this point forward we are to recognize Him not by physical sight but rather by hearing Him take, bless, break and give the bread to us? Until the end of time when Christ returns, His presence will be in the Eucharist and offered by the ordained priest who acts in the person of Christ.

The words of Pope Saint John Paul II about "Eucharistic amazement" are echoed in the words of Pope Benedict XVI who wrote about "Eucharistic wonder" in *Sacramentum Caritatis*.[3] In his apostolic exhortation the Holy Father wrote how the Eucharistic food is not changed into us, but rather, how we are transformed by Christ who through the Eucharist

---

2   John Paul II, Encyclical Letter *Ecclesia de Eucharistia*, April 17, 2003, n. 6.
3   Benedict XVI, *Sacramentum Caritatis*, Feb. 22, 2007, n. 97.

draws us to Himself.[4] All of this leads certainly to a sense of astonishment.

The spiritual guide Saint Ambrose lived in the fourth century. He tells us that we can marvel at the gift of bread and wine and be astonished that Christ's blessing consecrates what nature has formed. In Christ's blessing the nature of the bread and wine is transfigured, thus becoming the body and blood of Jesus. For Ambrose, the meaning of *transfigured* suggested that something ceased to be what it was and became what it had not previously been. That is what occurs during the Sacrifice of the Mass—the bread and wine are transfigured, ceasing to be what they had been and becoming what they previously were not. Ambrose stated the following:

> Jesus said, "For my Flesh truly is food and my Blood truly is drink." You hear of flesh, you hear of blood, and you are aware of the Sacraments of the Lord's death. For as often as we receive the Sacraments, which, through the Mystery of the sacred prayer, are transfigured into Flesh and Blood, "we announce the death of the Lord."[5]

****

To describe some stories as astonishing is an understatement. For example, in 2013 the host of the popular HGTV "Flip or Flop" program received a message from a registered nurse who, while watching the program, noticed a lump in the host's throat and emailed the show's producers to encourage the star to have a biopsy. He did so, and the results showed that he had thyroid cancer for which he underwent treatment. The nurse said that she had been watching the program and noticed the lump. She rewound the program and watched it again before contacting the producers. The television host said that he had seen a doctor earlier but was told that his condition was benign. Because of the insight given by the nurse who had been watching the program, the television host received treatment for thyroid cancer and was most grateful.

---

4   Ibid., 70.
5   Ambrose, *De Fide*, Book IV, 10, 124.

As astonishing as the previous story is, here's another. A New York based ear, nose and throat specialist was watching a television program on the HGTV channel when he noticed that a woman on the program had a small lump on her neck. He said that what he noticed was something that only a trained doctor would recognize as needing attention. The surgeon realized that the woman's condition was serious, but he had no idea who she was and the program did not mention her last name. In order to reach her, he turned to social media, posting a clip from the program that showed the woman, and asked if anyone knew how to get in touch with her. Eventually the doctor made contact with the young woman, who was from North Carolina, and told her that she needed a sonogram and a biopsy. She went to see a specialist, was diagnosed with thyroid cancer and subsequently received medical treatment. She and many others were astonished by the way in which her cancer was discovered and treated.

****

Summary statement:

Although we can remain amazed that God continues to love our sinful world and continues to hold us close to Himself in that love, the person of faith has to be astonished when considering how Jesus took the simple elements of bread and wine and chose them to be the means by which His Real Presence would remain with us until the end of time. Just as the bread and wine become transfigured, so also Jesus has become transfigured for us as the glorified and Risen Lord Jesus Christ.

For over a half century, every day, beginning on
2 November 1946, when I celebrated my first Mass in the
Crypt of the Cathedral in Krakow, my eyes have gazed in
recollection upon the host and the chalice, where time and
space in some way "merge" and the drama of Golgotha is
re-presented in a living way, thus revealing its mysterious
"contemporaneity." Each day my faith has been able to
recognize in the consecrated bread and wine the divine
Wayfarer who joined the two disciples on the road to
Emmaus and opened their eyes to the light
and their hearts to new hope.

Allow me, dear brothers and sisters, to share with deep
emotion, as a means of accompanying and strengthening
your faith, my own testimony of faith in the Most Holy
Eucharist. *Ave verum corpus natum de Maria Virgine,
vere passum, immolatum, in cruce pro homine!* Here is
the Church's treasure, the heart of the world, the pledge
of the fulfillment for which each man and woman, even
unconsciously, yearns. A great and transcendent mystery,
indeed, and one that taxes our mind's ability to pass
beyond appearances. Here our senses fail us: *visus, tactus,
gustus in te fallitur,* in the words of the hymn *Adoro Te
Devote;* yet faith alone, rooted in the word of Christ
handed down to us by the Apostles, is sufficient for us.
Allow me, like Peter at the end of the Eucharistic discourse
in John's Gospel, to say once more to Christ, in the name
of the whole Church and in the name of each of you:
"Lord, to whom shall we go?
You have the words of eternal life" (Jn 6:68).

Saint John Paul II, *Ecclesia de Eucharistia,* 59

Awareness

Are you **unaware** that we who were baptized into Christ Jesus were baptized into his death? We were indeed buried with him through baptism into death, so that, just as Christ was raised from the dead by the glory of the Father, we too might live in newness of life.

(Rom 6:3-4)

A while ago I was visiting with a parishioner who showed me a video of her great-grandson who seemed delighted with some of his newly-discovered abilities. The infant was about eight months old and was giggling and turning himself over as he rolled on the carpet in one of the rooms in the family home. Although the video camera was focused on the child, in the background the parents, by the intonation of their voices, were encouraging the little boy to keep turning over. Each time the child heard the encouraging tone of his parents' voices he responded with a giggle and with another turn of his body. He was becoming aware of the sound of encouragement and also becoming aware of what he could accomplish with his little body.

As we grow, we become aware of many things. We become aware of things we should do and things we should avoid. We become aware of what is acceptable and what is not. We become aware of the world around us and what we should do in a variety of situations. As we grow older we become aware of what insurance policies we should have, what medications we should take, what preparations we should make before we die. It seems that becoming aware is a lifelong project that culminates in an awareness of our finite nature and eventual death.

Our Blessed Mother became aware that God was calling her to a challenging task when she was asked to be the mother of the world's Savior. As time passed, she and Joseph must have become more aware of God's presence in their lives as they watched their Son grow in wisdom, age and grace. I'm sure that their awareness of Jesus' mission deepened greatly when they discovered Him in the Temple, sitting among the elders and debating with them.

As a Catholic I am aware that God's divine revelation culminates in the mystery of Jesus. When we participate in the liturgy we hear these words at the beginning of the Eucharistic Prayer: "Holy, holy, holy, Lord God of hosts. Heaven and earth are full of your glory." If we pray these words thoughtfully, we become aware of quite a bit. We are made aware that God is the Lord of heaven and earth and that both are filled with God's glory. Perhaps we might be aware that these words echo what Isaiah heard when he experienced a vision of angels proclaiming the praises of God (see Is 6:1-3). Isaiah began his prophetic ministry around the year 742 B.C. while praying in the Temple in Jerusalem. Isaiah's vision allowed him to become aware of and overwhelmed by the holiness of God and the sinfulness of humankind. Isaiah lived during the critical time of Israel's history when the northern kingdom collapsed in 722 B.C. After Isaiah's death, similar prophetic voices added their words about God's sovereign majesty and about human sin. These prophetic messages constitute the second and third sections of the Book of Isaiah.

Chapters 40-55, comprising the second section of the Book of Isaiah, are generally attributed to an anonymous prophet in the tradition of Isaiah. Within these chapters of second Isaiah we find the great oracles known as the Songs of the Suffering Servant. These four oracles are proclaimed every year during Holy Week, and the fourth Song of the Suffering Servant is read during the liturgy of Good Friday.

The third section from the Book of Isaiah contains oracles in the spirit of Isaiah. A very significant passage from Third Isaiah is proclaimed each year at the Chrism Mass (see Is

61:1-9) and relates to the identity of the Suffering Servant who would bring good news to the broken-hearted and who would bring about a spiritual renewal among the people.

In Luke's Gospel we find that Jesus began His public ministry after His temptation in the desert. He returned to Nazareth where He had grown up and entered the synagogue on the Sabbath. Here He found Himself rejected by His own hometown neighbors. Perhaps this was Luke's way of hinting that Jesus would also be rejected by a greater population of Israel at a future time. Nevertheless, Jesus entered the synagogue, where He was handed a scroll that contained the words from the Book of Isaiah (Is 61). After proclaiming the passage from Isaiah, Luke's Gospel indicates the following: "Rolling up the scroll, he handed it back to the attendant and sat down, and the eyes of all in the synagogue looked intently at him. He said to them, 'Today this scripture passage is fulfilled in your hearing'" (Lk 20:21). With these words Jesus was making His fellow Jews aware that the time for the fulfillment of the Old Testament hopes and expectations had now been inaugurated.

You might ask what this has to do with the theme of awareness—of our being aware that Christ is personally present in the Eucharist. The answer is this: Our awareness of how God's love has been given to us in the fullness of time is found in His Son, Jesus. We can summarize what has been said with the following points:

1. At the beginning of the Eucharistic Prayer, we pray the "Holy, holy, holy" which recalls the beginning of the prophetic mission of Isaiah.

2. In the Book of Isaiah we find the prophecies referring to the Suffering Servant, and those prophecies are fulfilled in Jesus.

3. In Luke's Gospel we hear that Jesus quoted the Prophet Isaiah at the beginning of His public ministry and stated that the prophecy was being fulfilled in Himself.

The first of the three preceding points indicates that the *Sanctus* of the Mass recalls the vision of Isaiah and the beginning of his prophetic ministry. The Chrism Mass, as indicated, contains the words of Isaiah with reference to the identity of the Suffering Servant. Finally, when the Fourth Eucharistic Prayer is invoked, we hear how the words of Isaiah (chapter 61) are incorporated within the prayer text. These are the words that we hear:

> *And you so loved the world, Father most holy,*
> *that in the fullness of time*
> *you sent your Only Begotten Son to be our Savior.*
> *Made incarnate by the Holy Spirit*
> *and born of the Virgin Mary,*
> *he shared our human nature*
> *in all things but sin.*
> *To the poor he proclaimed the good news of salvation,*
> *to prisoners, freedom,*
> *and to the sorrowful of heart, joy.*
> *To accomplish your plan,*
> *he gave himself up to death,*
> *and, rising from the dead,*
> *he destroyed death and restored life.*

Of what things do the words of the Eucharistic Prayer make us aware? First, the prayer speaks about God the Father's love for us by giving us His Son, Jesus, as our Savior. The prayer also makes us aware that Jesus was born in a miraculous way through the overshadowing of the Holy Spirit. We are also made aware that Jesus shared our human nature in all things but sin. Further, we become aware of Jesus' preaching and healing ministry which led to His death on the Cross. We are made aware that by Christ's Resurrection, death is destroyed and the promise of eternal life is restored. Finally, during the Eucharistic Prayer we become aware of the action of the Holy Spirit who transforms the elements of bread and wine into Christ's body and blood. All these things have the capacity to make us aware that when we receive Jesus in Holy Communion, we are receiving the most wonderful gift that God has bestowed upon humankind until the end of time when Christ will return in glory for the Final Judgment.

Saint Pius X, often referred to as the "Pope of the Eucharist," initiated reforms pertaining to the Eucharist which influenced the daily lives of Catholics in a significant way. At the time when he was elected pope in 1903, many Catholics received Holy Communion infrequently. This was due at least in part to the rise of Jansenism and its more stringent attitudes.[1] Pius X, in his 1910 encyclical *Quam Singulari*, wanted to promote an awareness of the importance of the frequent reception of Holy Communion and lowered the age for the reception of the sacrament to when a child reaches the ability to reason. This has been the practice ever since.

Pope Pius XII, in his encyclical *Haurietis Aquas*, wrote about the awareness of Christ's love that ought to penetrate every human heart. The encyclical specifically referenced the love of Jesus and of His Sacred Heart and how Christ's love continues to be shown in the Eucharist. He wrote:

> Even before He ate the Last Supper with His disciples, Christ Our Lord, since He knew He was about to institute the sacrament of His body and blood by the shedding of which the new covenant was to be consecrated, felt His heart roused by strong emotions, which He revealed to the Apostles in these words: "With desire have I desired to eat this Pasch with you before I suffer." And these emotions were doubtless even stronger when "taking bread, He gave thanks, and broke, and gave to them, saying, 'This is My body which is given for you; this do in commemoration of Me.' Likewise the chalice also, after He had supped, saying, 'This chalice is the new testament in My blood, which shall be shed for you.'"

> It can therefore be declared that the divine Eucharist, both the sacrament which He gives to men and the sacrifice in

---

1 One of the tenets of Jansenism was to discourage frequent reception of Holy Communion. Jansenists believed that to receive Holy Communion, one needed to have attained a high degree of spiritual perfection, including purification from all venial sin.

which He unceasingly offers Himself "from the rising of the sun till the going down thereof," and likewise the priesthood, are indeed gifts of the Sacred Heart of Jesus.[2]

A further awareness of Christ's presence in the Eucharist was given by Saint Paul VI in an address given in a General Audience in November of 1969. He said that the Holy Sacrifice of the Mass is a sacrifice offered by an ordained priest "in a different mode, that is, unbloodily and sacramentally, as his [Christ's] perpetual memorial until his final coming."[3]

I fully believe this. I believe that Jesus is sacramentally present in every tabernacle where His Real Presence is solemnly reserved. Because I believe that Christ is present in the Eucharist reserved in the tabernacle, I sometimes place a name or an intention inside the tabernacle as a sign of faith in Jesus. I am confident that He holds the person or the intention close to His Sacred Heart.

****

According to multiple reports, on a Friday in March of 2018, a man claiming to be acting for ISIS entered a supermarket in southern France. Minutes earlier the man had stolen a car after shooting the driver. He also fired his weapon on a group of policemen who then followed him to the supermarket. Witnesses remembered that when he entered the store he had been shouting that he was a soldier for the Islamic State. He immediately shot a worker and a customer, and then held all those in the supermarket as hostages, threatening to blow up the store and everyone inside. One of the military police officers, Lieutenant Colonel Arnaud Beltrame, began to speak with the attacker and was able to divert his attention while other police officers evacuated most of the others from the building. However, the attacker kept a woman hostage to serve as a human shield. Colonel Beltrame, in a gesture of heroism, offered himself in exchange for the civilian. He left his cell

2   Pius XII, Encyclical Letter *Haurietis Aquas*, May 15, 1956, nn. 70-71.
3   Paul VI, Address to a General Audience, November 26, 1969, *DOL* 212, 1762-63.

phone in an area that allowed the other police officers to hear what was occurring. After the exchange was made and in the hours that followed, shots were heard and the police stormed the building, killing the attacker whose connection with ISIS had been confirmed. Colonel Beltrame had a bullet wound in his neck and had also suffered mortal knife wounds to his throat. He was taken to a hospital where he died the following morning. However, in the intervening time while he was in the hospital he received not only the sacraments of Anointing of the Sick and the Eucharist but also Matrimony to the woman he had planned to marry two months later.

When the death was announced, Colonel Beltrame's mother was asked if she was proud of her son. She said that her son would have told her, "I'm doing my job, mum, that's all." She commented that he was always aware of the risk included with his work as a police officer. His brother further commented on Colonel Beltrame's awareness when he added that his brother "was well aware he had almost no chance. He was very aware of what he was doing."

Colonel Beltrame was only 44 years old, but in his lifetime he had served in Iraq for which he was given an award for bravery, was knighted in France's prestigious Legion of Honor and had been appointed as deputy commander of the anti-terror police in the region of southern France.

On the day of Colonel Beltrame's funeral, despite heavy rain, crowds lined the Paris roads as the funeral cortege made its way through the city. At his funeral the national chaplain of the police commented that the lieutenant colonel was a practicing Catholic and that he radiated his faith. He commented that Colonel Beltrame was always aware that his calling was to love God first and then to love his neighbor.

****

Summary statement:

The Eucharistic Prayer offered at Mass allows us to grow in our awareness that the life of the Suffering Servant as prophesied in the Book of Isaiah is fulfilled in Jesus. He is the one who gave Himself up to death, and rising from the grave, destroyed death and restored our life of grace with God the Father. Likewise, we become aware during the Mass that God's Holy Spirit is called upon to transform bread and wine into Our Lord's body and blood. When we become aware that the Real Presence of Christ in His glorified humanity is with us in sacramental form, we are better attuned to the divine companionship offered to us and to the promise of Christ who said He would not leave us orphaned.

With His word and with the elements of bread and wine, the
Lord himself has given us the essential of this new worship.
The Church, his Bride, is called to celebrate the Eucharistic
banquet daily in his memory. She thus makes the redeeming
sacrifice of her Bridegroom a part of human history and makes
it sacramentally present in every culture. This great mystery
is celebrated in the liturgical forms which the Church, guided
by the Holy Spirit, develops in time and space. We need a
renewed awareness of the decisive role played by the Holy
Spirit in the evolution of the liturgical form and the deepening
understanding of the sacred mysteries. The Paraclete, Christ's
first gift to those who believe, already at work in Creation, is
fully present throughout the life of the incarnate Word: Jesus
Christ is conceived by the Virgin Mary by the power of the
Holy Spirit; at the beginning of his public mission, on the banks
of the Jordan, he sees the Spirit descend upon him in the form
of a dove; he acts, speaks and rejoices in the Spirit, and he can
offer himself in the Spirit. In the so-called "farewell discourse"
reported by John, Jesus clearly relates the gift of his life in the
paschal mystery to the gift of the Spirit to his own. Once risen,
bearing in his flesh the signs of the passion, he can pour out the
Spirit upon them, making them sharers in his own mission. The
Spirit would then teach the disciples all things and bring to their
remembrance all that Christ had said, since it falls to him, as the
Spirit of truth, to guide the disciples into all truth. In the account
in Acts, the Spirit descends on the Apostles gathered in prayer
with Mary on the day of Pentecost and stirs them to undertake
the mission of proclaiming the Good News to all peoples.
Thus it is through the working of the Spirit that Christ himself
continues to be present and active in his Church, starting with
her vital center which is the Eucharist.

Benedict XVI, *Sacramentum Caritatis* 12

Attitude

Have among yourselves the same **attitude**
that is also yours in Christ Jesus,
Who, though he was in the form of God,
did not regard equality with God something to be grasped.
Rather, he emptied himself, taking the form of a slave,
coming in human likeness; and found human in
appearance, he humbled himself, becoming obedient to
death, even death on a cross.
Because of this, God greatly exalted him
and bestowed on him the name that is above every name,
that at the name of Jesus every knee should bend,
of those in heaven and on earth and under the earth,
and every tongue confess that Jesus Christ is Lord,
to the glory of God the Father.

(Phil 2:5-11)

Carlo Acutis was born in 1991. As the young Italian boy grew, he showed an aptitude for computer programming, and some considered him to be a computer "geek." He played soccer and for the most part was a typical teenager. However, he was atypical in his love for the Eucharist. After his First Communion, which he received early, he never missed attending daily Mass. He would often say that the Eucharist was his "highway to heaven." His love for the Eucharist prompted him to create a website where he catalogued the locations, dates and stories of various Eucharistic miracles.

In 2006 Carlo died as a result of an aggressive form of leukemia. He was only fifteen at the time. In October of 2020 the ceremony of his beatification occurred in Assisi, Italy. The Cardinal who presided at the liturgy said the following of Carlo: "He was an ordinary boy, simple, spontaneous, like-able ... he loved nature and animals, he played football, he had many friends ... and self-taught, he built websites to transmit the Gospel." In Carlo's brief life span he showed his love for Christ and wanted to live with the attitude of Christ. An example of this can be seen in the fact that he took the first paycheck he ever received to purchase a sleeping bag for a homeless man whom he noticed while walking to church. Although an ordinary boy in many ways, he displayed in an extraordinary way the attitude of Christ.

Saint Paul encouraged the Philippians to live in the attitude of Jesus, whom Paul declared to be the perfect man (see Phil 2:5). In his letter Saint Paul encouraged the young Christian community to love one another, to forgive the faults of others and to be of service to one another just as Christ has shown us. Likewise, in his words to the Corinthians (1 Cor 11:28-29) Saint Paul was explicit in his mandate that followers of Jesus should be marked by the attitude of Christ. He disapproved of any type of selfishness or unwillingness to share with those in need. Furthermore, he condemned their liturgical practice of coming together to celebrate the Eucharist while serious divisions existed among them. Paul was adamant in his concern that followers of Christ should have the attitude of Christ.

One of the intentions that I keep in mind when I spend time in prayer is for my attitude to conform to the attitude of Christ. I realize that, for that to happen, I also need to ask the Holy Spirit to remove any thoughts or desires which are contrary to Christ's attitude. Sometimes when I make that request of the Holy Spirit, I think of Michelangelo who chiseled pieces of stone, seeing in his mind the completed work. That's what I ask of the Holy Spirit—to keep chiseling away whatever is contrary to the attitude of Christ in me. In God's good time and with the grace of the Holy Spirit, I believe this can happen.

Saint John Paul II wrote the encyclical letter *Ecclesia de Eucharistia* in which he lamented the attitude that condones certain unacceptable Eucharistic practices and doctrines. For example, he wrote the following:

> In some places the practice of Eucharistic adoration has been almost completely abandoned. In various parts of the Church abuses have occurred, leading to confusion with regard to sound faith and Catholic doctrine concerning this wonderful sacrament. At times one encounters an extremely reductive understanding of the Eucharistic mystery. Stripped of its sacrificial meaning, it is celebrated as if it were simply a fraternal banquet. Furthermore, the necessity of the ministerial priesthood, grounded in apostolic succession, is at times obscured and the sacramental nature of the Eucharist is reduced to its mere effectiveness as a form of proclamation. This has led here and there to ecumenical initiatives which, albeit well-intentioned, indulge in Eucharistic practices contrary to the discipline by which the Church expresses her faith. How can we not express profound grief at all this? The Eucharist is too great a gift to tolerate ambiguity and depreciation.[1]

Several hundred years had passed from the time of Paul's letters to the writing of the first complete theological monograph on the Eucharist. This writing is attributed to Saint Paschasius Radbertus, who lived near the end of the 8th century. In his work, Paschasius reflected on the words of Saint Paul to the Corinthians and called upon Christians who wished to receive the precious gift of the Eucharist to live in the attitude of Christ. Similar to Saint Paul's concerns, Paschasius Radbertus reminded his fellow Christians to refrain from receiving the Eucharist unless and until they had Christ's attitude within them. His writing includes the following:

> What does the sinner eat and what does he drink? Not indeed the Flesh and Blood in a way that is for his profit, but rather judgment, even though it appears that he receives the Sacrament of the altar along with others ... For him the power of the Sacrament is withdrawn, and because of presumption his liability to judgment is doubled.[2]

---

1 John Paul II, Encyclical Letter *Ecclesia de Eucharistia*, n. 10.

2 Paschasius Radbertus, *De Corpore et Sanguine Domini*, p. 35. The quote is

Pope Pius XII wrote an encyclical on the sacred liturgy called *Mediator Dei*. In the encyclical, the Holy Father wrote about the attitude that should be within every person celebrating the Eucharistic sacrifice. He wrote:

> It is, therefore, desirable, Venerable Brethren, that all the faithful should be aware that to participate in the Eucharistic sacrifice is their chief duty and supreme dignity, and that not in an inert and negligent fashion, giving way to distractions and day-dreaming, but with such earnestness and concentration that they may be united as closely as possible with the High Priest, according to the Apostle, "Let this mind be in you which was also in Christ Jesus." And together with Him and through Him let them make their oblation, and in union with Him let them offer up themselves.[3]

Pius XII then addressed the attitude of Christ as well as the attitude that all Christians should possess. His words are sincere and moving:

> It is quite true that Christ is a priest; but He is a priest not for Himself but for us, when in the name of the whole human race He offers our prayers and religious homage to the eternal Father; He is also a victim for us since He substitutes Himself for sinful man. Now the exhortation of the Apostle, "Let this mind be in you which was also in Christ Jesus," requires that all Christians should possess, as far as is humanly possible, the same dispositions as those which the divine Redeemer had when He offered Himself in sacrifice: that is to say, they should in a humble attitude of mind, pay adoration, honor, praise and thanksgiving to the supreme majesty of God. Moreover, it means that they must assume to some extent the character of a victim and that they deny themselves as the Gospel commands, that freely and of their own accord they do penance and that each detests and satisfies for his sins. It means, in a word, that we must all undergo

found in James T. O'Connor's *The Hidden Manna: A Theology of the Eucharist* (Ignatius: San Francisco, 2005).

3   Pius XII, Encyclical Letter *Mediator Dei* 80, Nov. 20, 1947.

with Christ a mystical death on the cross so that we can apply to ourselves the words of St. Paul, "With Christ I am nailed to the cross."[4]

To conclude this segment of the meditation I will once again cite the words of Saint John Paul II in *Ecclesia de Eucharistia*. He writes not only about the attitude of Christ in giving us the Eucharist, but also about the attitude with which we should approach the Eucharist:

> When the Church celebrates the Eucharist, the memorial of her Lord's death and resurrection, this central event of salvation becomes really present and the work of our redemption is carried out. This sacrifice is so decisive for the salvation of the human race that Jesus Christ offered it and returned to the Father only after He had left us a means of sharing in it as if we had been present there. Each member of the faithful can thus take part in it and inexhaustibly gain its fruits. This is the faith from which generations of Christians down the ages have lived. The Church's Magisterium has constantly reaffirmed this faith with joyful gratitude for its inestimable gift. I wish once more to recall this truth and to join you, my dear brothers and sisters, in adoration before this mystery: a great mystery, a mystery of mercy. What more could Jesus have done for us? Truly, in the Eucharist, He shows us a love which goes "to the end" (cf. Jn 13:1), a love which knows no measure.[5]

****

Each year the Pope and his Roman Curia make a Lenten retreat. In the year 2000 when Pope John Paul II was serving the Church in his capacity as Roman Pontiff, he invited the Vietnamese Archbishop Francis Xavier Nguyen Văn Thuân to present the retreat reflections. The archbishop spoke about his years of arrest and imprisonment in various Communist prisons, several of them in solitary confinement. In the darkest moments during those years, he came to realize the one

---

4 Ibid., 81.
5 *Ecclesia de Eucharistia,* n. 11.

reason for us to hope. That one reason is Jesus Christ and the words that Christ has given to us in the Gospel. The archbishop focused his spiritual reflections around the need for a disciple of Christ to attain the attitude of Christ. The following is an excerpt from one of his talks.

> In prison I wrote, "Obey only one rule: the Gospel. This constitution is superior to all others. It is the rule that Jesus left to His apostles (cf. Mt 4:23). It is not difficult, complicated, or legalistic like the others. On the contrary, it is dynamic, kind, and invigorating for your soul. A saint who is far from the Gospel is a false saint."

> In fact, by entering us the Word of God questions our human ways of thinking and acting, and it introduces us to the new style of life inaugurated by Christ. For those who live the Gospel, it is possible to arrive, with Paul, at having "the mind of Christ" (cf. 1 Cor 2:16). It is also possible to acquire the capacity to read the signs of the times with the gaze of Christ Himself and, therefore, to creatively affect history; to experience true freedom, joy, and the courage of evangelical consistency; to find new faith in the Father with the rapport of authentic and sincere children; and to have a concrete and effective attitude of service toward all people.

> The Gospel, in short, awakens in us a profound sense of our life—we know finally why we are alive, and it makes us hope anew.

> The result is that it is no longer we who live, but Christ who comes to live in us. Through the words of Scripture, the Word makes his home in us and transforms us in *verba nel Verbo*, "word into the Word."[6]

****

Summary statement:

Central to the Christian life is for anyone baptized into Christ's life to also strive to grow in Christ's attitude. It is an attitude that helps us to navigate through the world around us. The attitude of Christ is the key—and is offered to us in Word

---

6 Francis Xavier Nguyen Van Thuan, *Testimony of Hope* (2001), 63-64.

and Sacrament. In the Gospels we hear about how Jesus comforted, consoled, challenged and loved. We are called to do the same. Receiving Our Lord in the Eucharist, the most august Sacrament, allows us to receive Christ's body, blood, soul and divinity—His life and attitude.

Behold, Lord, I cast my cares upon you so that I may live … You know my ignorance and my weakness; teach me and heal me. Your only Son, in whom are hidden all the treasures of wisdom and knowledge (cf. Col 2:3), redeemed me with his Blood … I ponder the price of my salvation, and I eat it and drink it and share it with others. Poor man that I am, I want to be filled with it in the company of those who eat and are satisfied.

Saint Augustine, *Confessions*, 10, 43

B

My meditation after receiving Holy Communion continues
with words or phrases beginning with the letter "B."

*Lord Jesus, I **believe** that You are truly present within the
consecrated **bread** which has been **blessed and broken**.
Through the eyes of faith I affirm that what I have received
is Your **Body and Blood**.*

****

Believe – Bread – Blessed and Broken – Body and Blood

****

Believe

Jesus said to him, "Have I been with you for so long a time
and you still do not know me, Philip? Whoever has seen
me has seen the Father. How can you say,
'Show us the Father'? Do you not **believe** that
I am in the Father and the Father is in me?
The words that I speak to you I do not speak on my own.
The Father who dwells in me is doing his works.
Believe me that I am in the Father and the Father is in me,
or else, **believe** because of the works themselves.
Amen, amen, I say to you, whoever **believes** in me will do
the works that I do, and will do greater ones than these,
because I am going to the Father."

(Jn 14:9-12)

One of the first things that a believer learns about God is His omnipresence. God's ability to be present everywhere is fundamental to His being. Another basic Christian belief is that God is Trinity—three Divine Persons—and as Trinity, all three are omnipresent. We then need to consider the human nature of Jesus. With the Incarnation of Jesus, God became present to us in a totally new and most intimate way without any diminishment of His divinity. God assumed in the divine Person of Jesus a human nature. A question we might ask is this: Where is the human nature of Jesus now? If in His divinity the Second Person of the Blessed Trinity is omnipresent, what about in His resurrected and glorified humanity?

We proclaim as a matter of faith that Jesus is fully God and fully man. In His human nature Jesus has a human soul and human flesh. In His divinity Jesus has always been God, but in His humanity, He was born in time. From that point on and for the rest of eternity, He is and ever shall be both human and divine. The resurrected and glorified humanity of Jesus Christ is in heaven, where His divine Personhood is united to His human body and soul.

Jesus Christ is everywhere as God. He is present everywhere in His power, His knowledge and His essence. In His human nature, however, He remains in heaven united to His divine Personhood, and He is also present on earth in the sacraments, most notably in the Eucharist. In other words, Jesus Christ in His resurrected and glorified humanity is now in heaven and is now in every tabernacle throughout the world where the Blessed Sacrament is reposed. In the reposed Sacrament Christ prays for us. He prays for the Church. He continues to intercede on our behalf. In addition to the tabernacles where Christ is reposed, He is also sacramentally present on every altar where the Holy Sacrifice of the Mass is offered. Thus, Christ's Real Presence in the Eucharist is a sacramental presence.

In the first part of *Sacramentum Caritatis*, Pope Benedict XVI's apostolic exhortation on the Eucharist as the source and summit of the Church's life, he writes about how the Eucharist is a mystery to be believed. He states the following:

> *"The mystery of faith!"* With these words, spoken immediately after the words of consecration, the priest proclaims the mystery being celebrated and expresses his wonder before the substantial change of bread and wine into the body and blood of the Lord Jesus, a reality which surpasses all human understanding. The Eucharist is a "mystery of faith" par excellence: "the sum and summary of our faith." The Church's faith is essentially a Eucharistic faith, and it is especially nourished at the table of the Eucharist. Faith and the sacraments are two complementary aspects of ecclesial life. Awakened by the preaching of God's word, faith is nourished and grows in the grace-filled encounter with the Risen Lord which takes place in the sacraments: "Faith is expressed in the rite, while the rite reinforces and

strengthens faith." For this reason, the Sacrament of the Altar is always at the heart of the Church's life: "Thanks to the Eucharist, the Church is reborn ever anew!" The more alive the Eucharistic faith of the People of God, the deeper is its sharing in ecclesial life in steadfast commitment to the mission entrusted by Christ to his disciples. The Church's very history bears witness to this. Every great reform has in some way been linked to the rediscovery of belief in the Lord's Eucharistic presence among his people.[1]

It is important to remember that Christ's Real Presence in the Eucharist is sacramental. Otherwise the misunderstanding that the Jews experienced (see John 6) and which led them to turn away from Jesus might also be our misunderstanding. In other words, when Jesus told the Jews that they were to eat His flesh and drink His blood, there was no thought of cannibalism on the part of Christ. However, that is certainly what those who rejected the words of Jesus thought. It was at the Last Supper, however, when Jesus revealed to His Apostles that they were receiving Him in a sacramental manner. This means that when the Apostles ate the bread that Jesus distributed and drank from the cup after Jesus proclaimed that these elements were His body and blood, the apostles were receiving Christ, but not with His physical properties that they had been able to see and touch. They received Christ, but not in His natural physical condition. Rather, they received Christ's body, blood, soul and divinity in the new and eternal covenant that He was establishing with them—and with us.

I mentioned that one of the first things a believer learns about God is His ability to be omnipresent. This is something we know *about* God. There is a difference between knowing *about* God and knowing *God* in a personal relationship. Similarly, there is a difference between knowing *about* Jesus Christ in the Eucharist and knowing *Jesus Christ* in the Eucharist.

---

1   *Sacramentum Caritatis,* n. 10. The three quotes mentioned within the paragraph refer respectively to paragraph 1327 of the *Catechism of the Catholic Church*, to *Propositio 16* and to the homily delivered by Pope Benedict XVI during the Mass of Installation on May 7, 2005.

It is like the difference between knowing about the recipe in order to make a delicious dessert and actually enjoying the dessert by savoring each bite.

The belief that we have in the Real Presence of the Lord in the Eucharist derives from Jesus' own words. The sixth chapter of the Gospel according to John is one of the most difficult chapters in the Bible. The chapter begins with a large crowd who were following Jesus and who witnessed His miracle of multiplying a few loaves of bread that fed them all. A little later Jesus addressed them with this admonition: "Do not work for food that perishes but for the food that endures for eternal life, which the Son of Man will give you. For on him the Father, God, has set his seal" (Jn 6:27).

Then they asked Jesus for a sign—perhaps something similar to the sign Moses gave their ancestors when manna fell from the sky. Jesus reminded them that it was God who gave the manna, the bread from heaven. When the disciples said that they wanted to have the bread that gives life to the world, Jesus said: "I am the bread of life; whoever comes to me will never hunger, and whoever believes in me will never thirst" (6:35). Jesus then said that He came down from heaven to do the will of His Father so that "everyone who sees the Son and believes in him may have eternal life" (6:40). Then to clarify or perhaps to add emphasis, Jesus said the following referring to Himself:

> This is the bread that comes down from heaven so that one may eat it and not die. I am the living bread that came down from heaven; whoever eats this bread will live forever; and the bread that I will give is my flesh for the life of the world. (50-51)

Jesus fed a multitude with bread. He also spoke about the manna, the bread that their Jewish ancestors ate in the desert. Nevertheless, although they ate the manna, their ancestors eventually died. Jesus said that He is the true bread of life come down from heaven, but unlike the ancestors who ate the manna but died, whoever eats of the true bread (Jesus) will never die. Of course, these words were difficult for many of the disciples to believe. Jesus never backed away from what He was saying that day, but as a result, many disciples no longer walked with Him. Jesus asked the Twelve if they also wanted to leave, and Peter, the spokesman for the group, confessed their belief in Him by saying, "Master, to whom shall we go? You have the words of eternal life. We have come to believe and are convinced that you are the Holy One of God" (6:68-69).

Some in Jesus' day chose to believe, while others chose not to do so. The same occurs today. Saint Cyril of Jerusalem, around 350 A.D., wrote the following:

> Do not, therefore, regard the Bread and Wine as simply that, for they are, according to the Master's declaration, the Body and Blood of Christ. Even though the senses suggest to you the other, let faith make you firm. Do not judge in this matter by taste, but—be fully assured by the faith, not doubting that you have been deemed worthy of the Body and Blood of Christ.[2]

When a person says "I believe," usually an intellectual assent has been given. For example, I learned in elementary science that the sun is at the center of our solar system. I believe this and give intellectual assent to this concept. However, when a person says "I believe" from a biblical perspective, not only is there intellectual assent but there is also a personal entrustment. In that sense, we believe "into" someone or something. An example here might be a husband who says to his wife, "I believe in you." He doesn't simply give intellectual assent about his wife's goodness, but there is also personal entrustment on his part. Another example: Suppose you meet a young woman studying to become a doctor. She is intelligent and passes all of her courses with excellent grades. Do you believe that she could become a doctor? From an intellectual point of view, most of us would believe that this woman has all of the requisite skills to practice medicine. However, let's say that you find out

2   Saint Cyril of Jerusalem, *Catechetical Lectures* 22 [Mystagogic 4].

something currently occurring in her personal life that you find disreputable. Do you still believe that she would be a good doctor? I may be able to give intellectual assent that the woman has the ability to become a doctor, but would I entrust my life into her care after finding out what I know? From the biblical point of view, belief includes not only intellectual assent but also personal entrustment into the other. With regard to Jesus' words about being the Bread of Life, some of the disciples did not believe. Those who did, however, not only gave an intellectual assent to what Jesus was saying but also trusted Him. "Lord, to whom shall we go? You have the words of eternal life." Those were words of personal entrustment.

****

On October 31, 2010, a woman entered the cathedral in Baghdad to tell the priest who had officiated at her wedding that she was pregnant and wanted a blessing for herself and for the child in her womb. The priest gave a blessing, but within a few moments the priest, the woman, the unborn child and about fifty others were killed when gunmen stormed the cathedral and accused the Christians of being infidels.

The remarkable fact of the story was that the following Sunday, many of the Christians who were at the cathedral the previous week and who had survived the attack returned to worship God once again. They walked past police barricades and military trucks. They passed various security checkpoints and were frisked for weapons. Because they believed in the Eucharistic presence of Jesus Christ, they returned. The church walls were marked with bullet holes. Bloodstains remained on the walls, the ceiling and floor. Inside the church the pews had been removed and in their place hundreds of candles were lit and were placed on the floor in the shape of a giant cross.

When a reporter asked a woman why she returned, she responded with these words: "We forgive them. We're not afraid. They gave us blood and we give them forgiveness." For this woman and for many others who returned to the church after the massacre, they allowed a place of destruction to be for them a place of hope. The courage that they showed by returning to the church where one week earlier family and friends had been killed was something that most of the world would consider almost unbelievable. But these people understood in a way that most of us never will—the forgiveness of Christ and the hope that He offers us are real. These folks believed in the presence of Christ among them and they returned for the Eucharist and for the nourishment that Christ gives in His Body and Blood.

****

Summary statement:

The dictionary indicates that to "believe" means to accept something as true. A slightly nuanced version of the word means that a person has faith in the reliability of the data that we hold as true. In other words, we trust that what we rely upon is true. Before we can believe or trust (entrust), knowledge is required. Once the knowledge is obtained, the mind is able to determine whether or not to believe. All of this leads to a formula: Knowledge + Belief + Trust (entrustment) = Faith.

Hence the Christian people often follow the lead of St. Thomas and sing the words: "Sight, touch and taste in Thee are each deceived; The ear alone most safely is believed. I believe all the Son of God has spoken; Than truth's own word, there is no truer token."

And St. Bonaventure declares: "There is no difficulty over Christ's being present in the sacrament as in a sign; the great difficulty is in the fact that He is really in the sacrament, as He is in heaven. And so believing this is especially meritorious."

Saint Paul VI, *Mysterium Fidei* 19-20

Bread

[The crowd] said to Him, "What sign can you do, that we
may see and believe in you? What can you do?
Our ancestors ate manna in the desert, as it is written:
'He gave them **bread** from heaven to eat.'" So Jesus said
to them, "Amen, amen, I say to you, it was not Moses who
gave the **bread** from heaven; my Father gives you the true
bread from heaven. For the **bread** of God is that which
comes down from heaven and gives life to the world."
So they said to him, "Sir, give us this **bread** always."
Jesus said to them, "I am the **bread** of life;
whoever comes to me will never hunger,
and whoever believes in me will never thirst."

(Jn 6:30-35)

As a child I looked forward to the times when I could
accompany my mother to the bakery. Often she'd ask for a
loaf of sliced bread. I was fascinated as I watched the loaf of
bread go through the bread slicer. During my high school years
I attended a minor seminary where each of the students had a
specific job to perform. I was delighted when I found myself
assigned to the kitchen crew—and specifically, to the job of
slicing the loaves of bread that the kitchen staff had prepared
for the dinner meal. I was so thoroughly fascinated by the
bread slicer that in sophomore speech class I gave a presentation on the invention of the bread slicing machine. I could tell
from the response of my classmates that their interest in the
bread slicer was significantly less enthusiastic than mine. The
yawns and blank stares were a good indication of that.

The bread slicer is symbolic for me. It reminds me of the
times I accompanied my mother to the bakery. It reminds me

of my seminary formation and some of the simple pleasures of those years. It also reminds me of the smell of freshly-baked bread—a smell of which it seems we can never get enough.

In the liturgy the bread is central. From the earliest of times, bread was the key. For example, from the writings of Saint Ignatius of Antioch we read the following:

> I am God's wheat and shall be ground by the teeth of wild animals. I am writing to all the churches to let it be known that I will gladly die for God if only you do not stand in my way. I plead with you: show me no untimely kindness. Let me be food for the wild beasts, for they are my way to God. I am God's wheat and shall be ground by their teeth so that I may become Christ's pure bread.[1]

Saint Ignatius of Antioch, according to tradition, was consecrated a bishop by the Apostle Peter. Saint Ignatius was the bishop of Antioch in Syria and he made it his goal to defend Christ and the teachings of Christ. He was wrongfully sentenced to death during the reign of the despicable Emperor Trajan because he refused to renounce the Christian faith. In the year 107 A.D. he was taken to Rome where he was to be devoured by wild beasts. As he journeyed with the soldiers who were guarding him, he wrote seven letters to various Christian communities. His letters provided encouragement as well as instruction. Of course, his letter to the Romans was highly inspirational as he compared himself to wheat that would be ground by the teeth of the wild animals so that he could become Christ's bread.

Some years later Saint Ambrose (333-397 A.D.) wrote the following about the bread:

> You may perhaps say: "My bread is ordinary." But that bread is bread before the words of the Sacraments; where the consecration has entered in, the bread becomes the flesh of Christ. And let us add this: How can bread be the Body of Christ? The answer is by the consecration. The consecration

---

1   Saint Ignatius of Antioch, *Letter to the Romans.*

takes place by certain words; by those of the Lord Jesus. Like all the rest of the things said beforehand, they are said by the priest; praises are referred to God, prayer of petition is offered for the people, for kings, for other persons; but when the time comes for the confection of the venerable Sacrament, then the priest uses not his own words but the words of Christ. Therefore it is the word of Christ that confects this Sacrament ... Before it is consecrated it is bread; but where the words of Christ come in, it is the Body of Christ. Finally, hear him saying: "All of you take and eat of this; for this is My Body." And before the words of Christ the chalice is full of wine and water; but where the words of Christ have been operative it is made the Blood of Christ, which redeems the people.[2]

In the three Synoptic Gospels we find that Jesus used the multiplication of bread for five thousand to describe the presence of the Kingdom of God. Further, in Matthew's and Mark's Gospels we encounter Jesus also feeding four thousand. Mark's Gospel presents the story in a way that indicates that the Apostles did not understand what Jesus was doing. When Jesus fed five thousand, He was providing primarily for the Jews (Mk 6:34-44). Twelve baskets of leftovers were collected, representing the twelve tribes of Israel. Shortly thereafter, Jesus left the predominantly Jewish territory and headed to a part of Israel where many of the Gentiles (non-Jewish) lived. In that locale Jesus fed four thousand by multiplying seven loaves of bread (Mk 8:1-9). After all had eaten there were seven baskets filled with leftovers that had been collected, representing the seven Gentile nations that surrounded Israel.

Now comes the perplexing part of the story. In the previous chapters of Mark's Gospel Jesus had been laying the groundwork for His proclamation that the Kingdom of God was at hand. He did this by preaching and performing miracles. After Jesus had fed the four thousand, some Pharisees objected to Jesus' proclamation about the arrival of God's kingdom. They argued with Jesus and demanded "a sign

2   Saint Ambrose, *The Sacraments,* 4.4.14; 4.5.23.

from heaven to test him" (Mk 8:11). The response that Jesus gave them was reminiscent of God's response to Moses when God said that although He had given signs of His protection to the Israelites while they were in Egypt and in the wilderness, they still demanded more and failed to obey Him (Nm 14:22). Then Jesus, along with the twelve Apostles, got into a boat and headed back to the other shore. Once they were in the boat and heading homeward, the Apostles indicated to Jesus that they had only one loaf of bread for the thirteen of them. Remember, at the multiplication of the loaves there were seven wicker baskets of leftovers—but apparently the Apostles failed to take more than one loaf of bread when they got into the boat.

Using the imagery of bread, Jesus tells the Apostles to "guard against the leaven of the Pharisees and the leaven of Herod" (Mk 8:15). The leaven (sometimes referred to as the yeast) referred to the spreading of veiled evil. In other words, there was some veiled evil that was present in the obstruction of the Pharisees to Jesus' proclaiming the indwelling of God's Kingdom. The Pharisees represented the spiritual leaders just as Herod represented the civil leadership. Both had their reasons to obstruct Jesus' message, so He warned His Apostles to beware of them. The Apostles were still perplexed, so Jesus recalled for them the feeding of the five thousand and the feeding of four thousand. Both times an abundance of bread was left over. Perhaps Jesus was telling the Apostles to be on guard against the yeast (the leaven) of those who were objecting to what He was doing. Rather, they should recall what they saw with their own eyes—an abundance of bread after feeding so many. In other words, they should stay close to Jesus and they would see the abundance of God's Kingdom as it would continue to be made known.

****

The name Omer Westendorf is well-known among Catholic musicians and authors today. Among his numerous accomplishments, he founded the World Library of Sacred Music and authored many English hymn texts following Vatican II. One of Westendorf's best-known works is the hymn *Gift of Finest Wheat* (also known as *You Satisfy the Hungry Heart),* composed in 1976 for the International Eucharistic Congress in Philadelphia. The lyrics lead one to meditate on the great gift of the Eucharist.

You satisfy the hungry heart
with gift of finest wheat;
Come give to us, O saving Lord,
the Bread of Life to eat.

As when the shepherd calls his sheep,
they know and heed his voice;
So when You call Your family, Lord,
we follow and rejoice.

With joyful lips we sing to You
our praise and gratitude,
That You should count us worthy, Lord,
to share this heavenly food.

Is not the cup we bless and share
the blood of Christ outpoured?
Do not one cup, one loaf, declare
our oneness in the Lord?

The mystery of Your presence, Lord,
no mortal tongue can tell:
Whom all the world cannot contain
comes in our hearts to dwell.

You give Yourself to us, O Lord,
then selfless let us be,
To serve each other in Your name
in truth and charity.[3]

****

---

3   Text: Omer Westendorf. Music: Robert E. Kreutz. © 1977, Archdiocese of Philadelphia. Published by International Liturgy Publications. Used with permission. All rights reserved.

Summary statement:

Bread is one of life's staple foods. It is food that is made of some grain that has been ground into flour, some water, and usually some leavening agent. For these elements to become bread they must be mixed together and baked. We read in Exodus 12:15-20 that the bread eaten at the Passover was unleavened. We further read in the Gospels how Jesus multiplied loaves of bread and how He used bread at the Last Supper. Bread was an important symbol in many cultures, often holding significance beyond simply its nutritional value. In Christianity, bread is the key element pertaining to the Eucharist.

And this food is called among us the Eucharist, of which no one is allowed to partake but the man who believes that the things which we teach are true, and who has been washed with the washing that is for the remission of sins, and unto regeneration, and who is so living as Christ has enjoined. For not as common bread and common drink do we receive these; but in like manner as Jesus Christ our Savior, having been made flesh by the Word of God, had both flesh and blood for our salvation, so likewise have we been taught that the food which is blessed by the prayer of His word, and from which our blood and flesh by transmutation are nourished, is the flesh and blood of that Jesus who was made flesh.

St. Justin Martyr, *First Apology*, Chapter 66

Blessed and Broken

While they were eating, he took bread, **said the blessing, broke it,** and gave it to them, and said,
"Take it; this is my body."
Then he took a cup, gave thanks, and gave it to them, and they all drank from it. He said, "This is my blood of the covenant, which will be shed for many. Amen, I say to you, I shall not drink again the fruit of the vine until the day when I drink it new in the kingdom of God." Then, after singing a hymn, they went to the Mount of Olives.

(Mk 14:22-26)

Saint Augustine reminded us that the Old Testament is revealed in the New Testament and that the New (Testament) is concealed in the Old (Testament). With that in mind, we can say that the biblical basis for the Real Presence of Christ in the Eucharist can be traced back to the Old Testament. Before doing that, however, it is helpful to recall something about Christian typology. In the New Testament, for example, Saint Paul calls Adam "the type of the one who was to come" (Rom 5:14). Saint Paul was saying that Adam was a "type" of Christ. In Greek the term derives from a noun that means a *hitting* or a *stamp* and referred to an impression that was stamped on a coin. Saint Paul's remark about Adam was to say that he was an image of the one who was to come, namely Christ.

In addition to Saint Paul's reference to Adam as a type of Christ found in Romans 5:14, we also find a similar reference in his Letter to the Corinthians. When Saint Paul speaks of Christ's victory over sin and death, he implies that sin was originally introduced by Adam. For this reason, Saint Paul calls Christ the "New Adam" who destroyed sin and death and made the redemption of humanity possible. These are Paul's words:

> But now Christ has been raised from the dead, the first-fruits of those who have fallen asleep. For since death came through a human being, the resurrection of the dead came also through a human being. For just as in Adam all die, so too in Christ shall all be brought to life. (1 Cor 15:20-22)

Biblical typology is a form of exegesis that allows the characters and the prophecies of the Old Testament to be fulfilled in the New Testament. The story of Jonah can be seen as a type of Christ, since Jonah emerged from a large fish three days after the fish had swallowed him. So too, Christ, after three days, emerged from the tomb in His glorious Resurrection from death.

Focusing our attention on the **blessed and broken** bread that we read about at the Last Supper, we can draw from three Old Testament types which prefigured the Eucharist: 1) Melchizedek, the priest-king; 2) the bread that was part of the Passover ritual as the Israelites departed from Egypt; and 3) the manna in the wilderness that the Israelites were given by God for their sustenance.

Melchizedek offered bread and wine to Abram (see Gn 14:18-20). Melchizedek is a type, an image, of Christ the King and the Eternal High Priest of the New Covenant. Melchizedek appears in the Old Testament as the king of Salem and recognizes a victory won by Abram, a victory which five other local kings could not achieve. In recognition of Abram's victory, Melchizedek prepared a feast and honored Abram by declaring him "blessed by God Most High" (14:19). Holding the bread and the wine while blessing Abram, Melchizedek gave blessing to God for the victory over His foes, for the celebration in Abram's honor and for the courage Abram had shown. Although the Genesis story does not specifically say that the bread was blessed and broken, we can readily assume that a blessing was given by Melchizedek who was both king and priest. The bread and wine, once blessed, were consumed. This, of course, would mean that the blessed bread was then broken and distributed.

As priest-king, Melchizedek is introduced as one who believed in and was faithful to God. He was from Salem, which later became Jerusalem. His name means "king of righteousness" and his act of bringing bread and wine for Abram has led Scripture scholars to say that Melchizedek was a type of Christ. In Psalm 110 we read how God promised a priest-king who would have "princely power from the day of your birth" and who was begotten "in holy splendor" (110:3). The priest-king would also be "a priest forever in the manner of Melchizedek" (110:4). We find in the Letter to the Hebrews the following with reference to Melchizedek as a type of Christ:

> It was not Christ who glorified himself in becoming high priest, but rather the one who said to him: "You are my son; this day I have begotten you;" just as he says in another place: "You are a priest forever according to the order of Melchizedek." In the days when he was in the flesh, he offered prayers and supplications with loud cries and tears to the one who was able to save him from death, and he was heard because of his reverence. Son though he was, he learned obedience from what he suffered; and when he was made perfect, he became the source of eternal salvation for all who obey him, declared by God high priest according to the order of Melchizedek (Heb 5:5-10).

Righteousness is attributed to Jesus in several places in the New Testament. For example, in 1 Corinthians we read that in Jesus we have "righteousness, sanctification and redemption" (1:30) and from the Acts of the Apostles we read that Peter, speaking to the Jews, said: "You denied the Holy and Righteous One and asked that a murderer be released to you" (3:14). Thus, Melchizedek, the king of righteousness, can be considered as the type of Christ that we find in the New Testament.

With regard to the second of the Old Testament types, we can recall the tenth plague mentioned in the Old Testament

account of how the Passover feast originated. In the story of
the tenth plague, the unblemished lamb that was to be slain and
consumed became the type of Christ, the Lamb of God who
was crucified and who asked us to consume His flesh. Even
though the lamb is the type of Christ, we can also focus on the
bread. Since their departure from Egypt was abrupt, the people
had little time to prepare. The bread was to be unleavened (Ex
12:8) which allowed for the bread to bake more quickly since
there was no time for the bread to rise with the use of leavening ingredients. According to Exodus 12:8 the lamb and the
bread were to be eaten. After giving the instruction of how the
Passover would be a day of remembrance for future genera-
tions, Moses told the Israelites that in the future they would eat
unleavened bread for seven days with their houses cleared of
all leaven. Certainly the unleavened bread, given the emphasis
that Moses was placing upon it, was significant. After Moses
told the Israelites about how they must observe this rite each
year, he said,

> When your children ask you, "What does this rite of yours
> mean?" you will reply, "It is the Passover sacrifice for
> the Lord, who passed over the houses of the Israelites in
> Egypt; when he struck down the Egyptians, he delivered our
> houses" (12:26-27).

Having heard these words of Moses, the Israelites knelt
down, bowed their heads in worship, and then did what the
Lord had told them to do through the words of Moses (see
12:28). In other words, at that moment they blessed and broke
the unleavened bread and ate it with the roasted lamb.

The third Old Testament reference to blessed and broken
bread occurs when God provided manna in the wilderness due
to the grumbling of the Israelites. We read that the Lord spoke
to Moses and instructed him to tell the Israelites that God had
heard their grumbling and that "in the morning you will have
your fill of bread, and then you will know that I, the Lord, am
your God" (Ex 16:12). When the morning came, something
like "cakes of hoarfrost" were on the ground. The Israelites

asked what it was (in Hebrew, *man hu*) to which Moses responded: "It is the bread which the Lord has given you to eat" (16:15). Having heard through the words of Moses that the bread was from God, we can assume that they blessed and broke the bread each day. The story of the manna concludes with this thought: "The Israelites ate the manna for forty years, until they came to settled land; they ate the manna until they came to the borders of Canaan" (16:35).

From the New Testament we read about the bread blessed and broken at the Last Supper (see Lk 22:19). Luke uses a form of the Greek ευχαριστεο to describe when Jesus said the blessing. In essence, the blessing was one of thanksgiving. When Jesus broke the bread, He was fulfilling the prescribed Passover ritual. When early Christians gathered to celebrate the Eucharist, they commonly referred to it as the "breaking of the bread" (cf. Acts 2:42, 46; 20:7, 11).

In addition to the Last Supper's reference to the bread blessed and broken, we also find it in the narrative depicting the appearance of the Risen Lord on the road to Emmaus. We read: "And it happened that, while he was with them at table, he took bread, said the blessing, broke it, and gave it to them" (Lk 24:30). The resemblance of this passage to the Last Supper narrative is easily recognized. Just as Jesus opened the eyes of the two disciples in the breaking of the bread, the same can occur for us each time we share in the Eucharist, the breaking of the bread.

In the life of Jesus Himself, specifically in His public ministry, the Bread (Jesus) began His public life with His baptism in the Jordan by John. The voice of God the Father (see Lk 3:22) blessed His beloved Son, the future Bread of life. At the end of His public ministry in His baptism by blood upon the Cross, the Bread of life was broken. Therefore, the Bread (Jesus) was blessed and broken—blessed at the beginning of His public ministry and broken at its conclusion.

****

It's easy to take each day for granted. Many parents send their children off in the morning, perhaps to school or maybe to some other activity, without thinking too much about what a blessing they have in their child. Several years ago at the parish where I currently serve as pastor, two young girls died in a car accident. The visitation for the girls occurred in the church; hundreds of mourners came to offer support and condolences to the bereaved family. I was standing by one of the doors where many were exiting after paying their respects. One man, the father of a young boy and girl, said to me as he left the church that he was going home immediately to kiss his children and to tell them how much he loved them. From the broken hearts that he encountered during the visitation he realized all the more the blessing of his own children.

I mention this story because it is an example of being blessed and broken. The parents of the two girls who died were blessed to have their daughters as part of their lives. They also became broken in a matter of seconds when the girls were killed. Being blessed but also broken occurs in all of our lives. More often than not, we focus upon what is broken while taking the blessing for granted—or in some cases, not recognizing the blessing at all.

In recent months a story about being blessed and broken occurred in Alabama. A 13-year-old boy was admitted to a hospital after suffering a head injury—he was treated for seven skull fractures. The doctors who worked with the boy declared that he was brain-dead and were going to remove his life support. On the day before this was scheduled to happen, however, some indications of consciousness were recognized. During the previous week the boy had been unconscious and on a few occasions his heart needed to be resuscitated. However, in what can only be called a blessing that came after being broken, the boy woke up and began speaking. This is an example of realizing the blessing after being broken.

A third example of being both blessed and broken was given to me by one of the seminarians from our diocese. He had been speaking with another person who relayed the story about how a young man who was preparing for marriage asked both his mother and father what each regretted most in their marriage. He thought that by asking his parents what they regretted, he might be better prepared for the challenges of marriage. The young man's father said that he most regretted not being able to spend more time with his wife. The young man's mother said that she most regretted her sharp tongue and how she sometimes used it to speak poorly of her husband.

As it turned out, in time the young man's mother suffered a stroke which pretty much immobilized her and curtailed her ability to speak. Her husband, now retired, took this as an opportunity to be with her and to care for her night and day. He lifted her when she required being lifted. He clothed her, fed her, and gave her loving care. His comment, when asked about the care he gave his wife, was to indicate that the time they were spending together was a real blessing. Some would consider the wife's inability to speak as a broken-ness. She, however, saw it as a blessing because it curbed her sharp tongue. The same was true of the wife's stroke which prompted the husband to be with her around the clock. The broken-ness of her infirmity was a blessing for the husband since he could spend every waking and sleeping moment with his wife. They received a blessing, but it came at the price of being broken.

****

Summary statement:

When we receive the Eucharist at Mass, the bread is first blessed during the consecration and then broken during the fraction rite. The consecrated bread becomes for us the Bread of Life, Jesus Himself. The consecrated bread, blessed and broken at Mass, represents the full humanity of Jesus who also was blessed and broken in His public life and ministry. We who are also blessed and broken by events in our lives are thus able to unite those moments with Christ when we receive the Holy Eucharist, the Real Presence of Jesus, blessed and broken for us.

After the type had been fulfilled by the Passover
celebration and He had eaten the flesh of the lamb with
His apostles, He takes bread which strengthens the heart of
man, and goes on to the true Sacrament of the Passover,
so that just as Melchizedek, the priest of the Most High
God, in prefiguring Him, made bread and wine an offering,
He too makes Himself manifest in the reality
of His own Body and Blood.

St. Jerome, *Commentaries on Matthew* 4:26:26

Body and Blood

The Jews quarreled among themselves, saying,
"How can this man give us [his] flesh to eat?"
Jesus said to them, "Amen, amen, I say to you,
**unless you eat the flesh of the Son of Man
and drink his blood,** you do not have life within you.
Whoever eats my flesh and drinks my blood has eternal
life, and I will raise him on the last day.
For **my flesh is true food, and my blood is true drink.**
Whoever eats my flesh and drinks my blood remains
in me and I in him. Just as the living Father sent me
and I have life because of the Father, so also the one
who feeds on me will have life because of me.
This is the bread that came down from heaven.
Unlike your ancestors who ate and still died,
whoever eats this bread will live forever."

(Jn 6:52-58)

It has already been stated that in Hebrews 5:5-6 we read
that God the Father bestowed upon His Son an eternal priestly
kingship. The author writes:

> It was not Christ who glorified himself in becoming high
> priest, but rather the one who said to him: "You are my son;
> this day I have begotten you"; just as he says in another
> place: "You are a priest forever according to the order of
> Melchizedek."

Melchizedek was both a priest and a king. In Genesis we
read the following: "Melchizedek, king of Salem, brought out
bread and wine. He was a priest of God Most High" (14:18).

Because Jesus is referred to as the eternal priest-king
according to the order of Melchizedek, the bread and wine

become important symbols for what was to occur about 1800 years later when Jesus celebrated the Passover with His disciples at the Last Supper. He performed the Passover ritual in what had once been the region of Salem; that night it was known as the city of Jerusalem.

Bread and wine also have importance in some of the miracle stories about Jesus. He took bread and multiplied it in order to feed a hungry crowd. At a wedding in Cana He changed water into wine. Then, at the Last Supper, the greatest miracle occurred when Jesus took bread and wine and they became His body and blood that would be offered the following day for our redemption.

Jesus instituted the Eucharist as the lasting memorial of His death and Resurrection when He told His disciples to "do this in remembrance of me." His Apostles would become the priests of the new and eternal covenant. The *Catechism of the Catholic Church* reminds us that "At the heart of the Eucharistic celebration are the bread and wine that, by the words of Christ and the invocation of the Holy Spirit, become Christ's Body and Blood" (para. 1333). We also read in the same paragraph that "The Church sees in the gesture of the king-priest Melchizedek, who 'brought out bread and wine,' a prefiguring of her own offering."

When Jesus told His disciples (Jn 6:53) that they were to "eat His flesh" and "drink His blood," some argued that Jesus was speaking figuratively rather than literally. There are a number of compelling reasons to reject this idea. When we look at the context of where this passage is within the Johannine Gospel, we find that just before Jesus told the disciples to "eat His flesh" and "drink His blood," He had multiplied loaves of bread allowing more than 5000 to be fed (Jn 6:6). The miracle of feeding 5000 was an actual event, something which literally occurred. In placing this passage immediately before His words about "eating His flesh" and "drinking His blood," John's Gospel would be remiss to move from a literal event to one in which only figurative language was used.

A second reason for the literal meaning of the words is that when Jesus spoke about the manna that had been given to the disciples' ancestors, Jesus said that although the manna was eaten, those who ate it died. Jesus stated that the bread that He was giving would allow them to eat and not die (Jn 48-50). The manna from heaven was a literal occurrence; the "bread that comes down from heaven so that one may eat it and not die" could surely be no less literal.

If the disciples had not thought that the words of Jesus were literal, they would not have departed from Him. Similarly, if Jesus were speaking only figuratively, He would not have let them leave without trying to persuade them that He had been speaking in merely figurative language. For example, in John 11:11-14 we read about the raising of Lazarus. Jesus had said:

> "Our friend Lazarus is asleep, but I am going to awaken him." So the disciples said to him, "Master, if he is asleep, he will be saved." But Jesus was talking about his death, while they thought that he meant ordinary sleep.

From this passage we see that Jesus was clear about when He was using figurative language and when His words were literal.

Perhaps the best insight into the truth that Jesus was speaking literally at that moment comes from the Aramaic language itself. At the time of Jesus, the phrase "to eat the flesh" or "to drink the blood" of another had the symbolic meaning of persecution and bringing the other person to destruction. For example, we read the following in Isaiah 49:23b-26:

> Then you shall know that I am the Lord; none who hope in me shall be ashamed. Can plunder be taken from a warrior, or captives rescued from a tyrant? Thus says the Lord: Yes, captives can be taken from a warrior, and plunder rescued from a tyrant; those who oppose you I will oppose, and your sons I will save. I will make your oppressors eat their own flesh, and they shall be drunk with their own blood. All flesh shall know that I, the Lord, am your savior, your redeemer, the Mighty One of Jacob.

If the words of Jesus about "eating His flesh" and "drinking His blood" were symbolic rather than literal, He would have been suggesting that His disciples persecute and destroy Him. Therefore, a literal meaning has always been the way that the Catholic Church has explained this passage.

There is still a question to be answered. In the Book of Leviticus we read that the Lord told the following to Moses:

> As for anyone, whether of the house of Israel or of the aliens residing among them, who consumes any blood, I will set myself against that individual and will cut that person off from among the people, since the life of the flesh is in the blood, and I have given it to you to make atonement on the altar for yourselves, because it is the blood as life that makes atonement. That is why I have told the Israelites: No one among you, not even a resident alien, may consume blood. (Lv 17:10-12)

This was one of the Mosaic laws that received special emphasis. Thus the question remains as to how Jesus, a first-century Jewish man who was steeped in the knowledge of the Old Testament, could ask His disciples to do something that was considered to be vile and repulsive.

Dr. Brant Pitre addresses that question. He writes the following with regard to the misunderstanding of the disciples who were hearing Jesus' words and judging simply from appearances (like the manna of old) rather than from the supernatural bread that was to lead them to eternal life:

> Just as the Pharisees rejected Jesus because they did not recognize his supernatural origin but instead judged him only according to his appearance, so, too, Jesus' disciples did not believe his Eucharistic teaching because they didn't understand the supernatural nature of the new manna from heaven. They judged it only by its appearances. They didn't understand that he wished to give them his resurrected body and blood, miraculously present under the veil of bread and wine.[1]

---

1   Pitre, 114.

Dr. Pitre continues with a clear response to the question of how Jesus could ask His disciples to drink His blood. He writes:

> Last but not least, only when we grasp this connection between the new manna from heaven and Jesus' risen body are we able to explain his startling command to drink his blood (Jn 6:53-56). How could Jesus say such a thing when the Old Testament explicitly forbade the Israelites to drink the blood of an animal? I suggest that the very reason God forbids drinking blood in the Old Covenant is the same reason Jesus commands his disciples to drink his blood: "For the life [Hebrew *nephesh*] of the flesh is in the blood" (Lv 17:11). Jesus would have known the Law of Moses, and he would have known that the power of his own resurrected "life"—indeed, his "soul"—was in his blood. Therefore, if the disciples wished to share in the "life" of Jesus' bodily resurrection, then they had to partake of both his body and his blood. If they wanted a share in the life of his bodily resurrection, then they had to receive his blood, given to them as drink: "Unless you eat the flesh of the Son of man, and drink his blood, you have no life in you; he who eats my flesh and drinks my blood has eternal life, and I will raise him up on the last day" (Jn 6:54).[2]

The Law of Moses has served and still serves an important purpose. However, we recall Jesus' words when He said that He came not to abolish but to fulfill the Law (see Mt 5:17). In giving us His flesh to eat and blood to drink, Jesus was showing us that the Law of Love, the fullness of God's life to be offered in our own resurrection at the end of time, would be our reason to drink of His blood.

****

Matthew Kelly presents a compelling story in his book entitled *Rediscovering Catholicism*[3] where he describes the fictional outbreak of a never-seen-before flu virus that begins

---

2   Ibid., 115.
3   Matthew Kelly, *Rediscovering Catholicism* (Beacon Publishing: Boston, 2010), Prologue.

to take the lives of several people in India. Within days the flu has spread to Europe and finally to the United States. As the flu continues to take the lives of many individuals, an encouraging announcement is made. Doctors have found a cure and have the ability to create a vaccine. However, it will require a very special type of blood. Throughout the country everyone is required to go to a nearby hospital and have his or her blood tested.

One family—a husband, wife and children—have their blood tested. As they wait for the results, a medical team rushes toward them. The medical staff indicates to the parents that their son is a perfect match for the vaccine. The parents are asked to sign a statement allowing the technicians to extract the blood from the boy's body. The parents ask how many pints will be taken—and that is when an old doctor says, "We are going to need it all." Although the parents are horrified by what they hear, they sign the form because they know it is the only thing that will save the lives of many others. They sacrifice their son's body and blood for the sake of all humanity.

****

Summary statement:

Many Pharisees rejected Jesus because they judged Him by external appearances and not through the eyes of faith. Many of the disciples of Jesus left Him when He spoke about eating His body and drinking His blood for the same reason—they judged His words by external appearance rather than understanding the supernatural reality He was presenting. Christians are accustomed to looking beyond appearances. We see a picture of the babe in the manger and yet we are able to understand that this Child is God. Similarly, when we hear the words "This is my Body; this is my Blood," we move beyond the appearances of bread and wine, and our faith allows us to speak the words of Thomas the Apostle, "My Lord and my God."

According to the Fathers of the Church, the Eucharist must
be thought of as a certain continuation and extension of
the Incarnation. Through it, the substance of the incarnate
Word is linked with individual men and women, and,
in an admirable manner, the supreme sacrifice of Calvary
is renewed, as was foretold by the prophet Malachi,
"In every place a clean oblation is sacrificed
and offered to my Name." This miracle,
the very greatest of its kind, is accompanied by
innumerable miracles, for here all the laws of nature are
suspended. The whole substance of bread
and wine is converted into the Body and Blood of Christ;
the appearances of bread and wine, subjects
of no reality, are sustained by divine power.

Leo XIII, Encyclical *Mirae Caritatis* 8

C

The prayer after Communion continues with the letter "C" and words associated with it:

*Lord Jesus, in this **celebration of faith** I have received the **cup of blessing**. It is the new and eternal **covenant** of your love. May I proclaim once again this day that You are the **Christ**, the Anointed One of God who has come to me. Amen.*

****

Celebration – Cup – Covenant – Christ

****

Celebration of Faith

While he was still a long way off, his father caught sight
of him, and was filled with compassion. He ran to his
son, embraced him and kissed him. His son said to him,
"Father, I have sinned against heaven and against you;
I no longer deserve to be called your son." But his father
ordered his servants, "Quickly bring the finest robe and put
it on him; put a ring on his finger and sandals on his feet.
Take the fattened calf and slaughter it.
Then let us **celebrate** with a feast, because this son
of mine was dead, and has come to life again;
he was lost, and has been found."
Then the **celebration** began.

(Lk 15:20b-24)

When most people hear of a celebration, they often think
of some festive gathering. Most celebrations include food,
drink, laughter, merriment, and so on. Some celebrations are
casual while others are formal. Celebrations occur among the
young and the old and usually occur at key moments. Births
and birthdays, weddings, graduations, promotions, recovery
from injury, financial gain, holidays, special achievements and
recognitions—these are just a few of the many types of celebrations. These kinds of celebrations are enjoyable and filled
with social activity.

How can we call the Eucharist a celebration if in fact we
are renewing the sacrifice of Calvary? The basic response to
the question is that when we gather to pray the Eucharist, the
Paschal Mystery of Christ is celebrated and there is an out-
pouring of the Holy Spirit to make present what occurred at

Calvary. In other words, the Paschal Mystery is renewed—and that is cause for celebration as the Holy Spirit comes upon the gifts of bread and wine to transform them, and also as the Holy Spirit comes upon us to transform us into the Mystical Body of Christ.

The *Catechism of the Catholic Church* speaks about the celebration of the sacraments. In paragraph 1234 and referring to Baptism, the *Catechism* states that "The meaning and grace of the sacrament of Baptism are clearly seen in the rites of its celebration." It goes on to say that following the words and the gestures of the ceremony, "the faithful are initiated into the riches this sacrament signifies and actually brings about in each newly baptized person." The rituals include the Sign of the Cross, the reading of the Word of God, the baptismal water, the anointing with sacred chrism, the white garment, the candle and the solemn blessing. The *Catechism* includes the same basic ritual outline for each of the sacraments (for Confirmation, beginning with para. 1297; for Eucharist, para. 1345; for Reconciliation, para. 1480; for the Anointing of the Sick, para. 1517; for Holy Orders, para. 1572; for Matrimony para. 1621).

Ultimately, every liturgical celebration has the life of the Kingdom as its goal. Similar to the civic celebrations mentioned above (birthdays, etc.), liturgical celebrations are ritualized at key moments. We often include as part of the liturgical celebration some of the aforementioned activities. For example, most sacraments include a gathering of folks, some food and drink, and time for social interaction. Whether it is a celebration of Baptism or of a Christian funeral, the goal remains the same: life in the Kingdom of God. That is a worthy cause for celebration.

At the Last Supper Jesus and His apostles were celebrating the Passover. That is when the apostles received Christ's body and blood for the first time. However, this was already prefigured in the wedding feast at Cana. At that celebration Jesus took water and changed it into wine (see Jn 2:1-11).

Although procuring wine was the task of the bridegroom, the wedding celebration at Cana implied that the true Bridegroom was Jesus Himself. A hint to remind us that the bridegroom was responsible for obtaining the wine is suggested when the chief steward went to the Cana bridegroom and complimented him on saving the best wine until last. The true Bridegroom remained anonymous at that moment. His wedding union with humankind would come at a later time—upon the Cross.

The Eucharist is also prefigured when a few loaves and fish were multiplied and many were fed (see Jn 6:1-15). Being provided with nourishment was a reason for celebration. However, even more significant than the miracle of multiplying food was the fact that Jesus was leading His disciples in the way of faith. With the miracle of the loaves and fish Jesus was able to ignite the faith of His disciples. Perhaps with faith in the miracle that He performed with the loaves and fish, they might understand the greater miracle that was to occur. However, many of the disciples did not understand. Here is what the Gospel of John tells us:

> And when they found him across the sea they said to him, "Rabbi, when did you get here?" Jesus answered them and said, "Amen, amen, I say to you, you are looking for me not because you saw signs but because you ate the loaves and were filled. Do not work for food that perishes, but for the food that endures for eternal life, which the Son of Man will give you. For on him the Father, God, has set his seal." So they said to him, "What can we do to accomplish the works of God?" Jesus answered and said to them, "This is the work of God—that you believe in the one he sent." So they said to him: "What sign can you do, that we may see and believe in you? What can you do? Our ancestors ate manna in the desert, as it is written: 'He gave them bread from heaven to eat.'"

> So Jesus said to them, "Amen, amen, I say to you, it was not Moses who gave the bread from heaven; my Father gives you the true bread from heaven. For the bread of God is

74 The Medicine of Immortality

that which comes down from heaven and gives life to the world." (Jn 6:25-33)

Because of a lack of faith, many of the disciples rejected what Jesus was telling them. However, even this was cause for celebration, because after many of the disciples left and Jesus turned to ask His disciples if they also wanted to leave Him, Simon Peter answered Jesus by saying: "You have the words of eternal life. We have come to believe and are convinced that you are the Holy One of God" (Jn 6:68-69). Why would there be celebration at that moment? Jesus knew that He could entrust the Church that He was establishing to the guidance and care of Simon Peter. Furthermore, this Scripture passage is cause for celebration because it is here that the Eucharistic theme comes to the foreground.

Pope Benedict XVI, in the second part of his apostolic exhortation *Sacramentum Caritatis*, writes about the Eucharist as a mystery to be celebrated. He writes:

> The Synod of Bishops reflected at length on the intrinsic relationship between Eucharistic faith and Eucharistic celebration, pointing out the connection between the *lex orandi* and the *lex credendi*, and stressing the primacy of the liturgical action. The Eucharist should be experienced as a mystery of faith, celebrated authentically and with a clear awareness that the *"intellectus fidei* has a primordial relationship to the Church's liturgical action."[1]

Pope Benedict XVI further commented on the *ars celebrandi* (the art of celebration) in these words:

> In the course of the Synod, there was frequent insistence on the need to avoid any antithesis between the *ars celebrandi*, the art of proper celebration, and the full, active and fruitful participation of all the faithful. The primary way to foster the participation of the People of God in the sacred rite is the proper celebration of the rite itself. The *ars celebrandi* is the best way to ensure their *actuosa participatio*. The *ars celebrandi* is the fruit of faithful adherence to the liturgical

1 *Sacramentum Caritatis* 34, citing the *Relatio post disceptationem*, 4.

norms in all their richness; indeed, for two thousand years this way of celebrating has sustained the faith life of all believers, called to take part in the celebration as the People of God, a royal priesthood, a holy nation.[2]

Throughout the second part of *Sacramentum Caritatis* Pope Benedict XVI takes us through the proper way to celebrate the Holy Mass. He addresses the proper respect that should be given to liturgical books and the richness of liturgical signs, the beauty of liturgical song, and then he points to the structure of the Eucharistic celebration itself. Underlying each of these themes is the interior disposition that each person should have towards his or her active participation in the Eucharistic celebration. The Holy Father writes:

> I am thinking in general of the importance of gestures and posture, such as kneeling during the central moments of the Eucharistic Prayer. Amid the legitimate diversity of signs used in the context of different cultures, everyone should be able to experience and express the awareness that at each celebration we stand before the infinite majesty of God, who comes to us in the lowliness of the sacramental signs.[3]

One of the earliest of Eucharistic celebrations recorded in the Bible occurred when Jesus encountered two disciples on their journey to Emmaus (see Lk 24:13-35). When you read or hear the story, what is your image of the two disciples? Do you immediately think of two men? We know that one of the disciples was named Cleopas (24:18) but what about the other? Might it have been Cleopas' wife? Given that they were heading home and they both invited Jesus to stay with them, could they have been a husband and wife?

The real point of the story is that the two disciples recognized Jesus in the breaking of the bread (24:30), and recognizing Him, they were celebrating. Here is what we read:

> With that their eyes were opened and they recognized him, but he vanished from their sight. Then they said to each

2   Ibid., 38.
3   Ibid., 65.

other, "Were not our hearts burning [within us] while he spoke to us on the way and opened the scriptures to us?" So they set out at once and returned to Jerusalem where they found gathered together the eleven and those with them who were saying, "The Lord has truly been raised and has appeared to Simon!" Then the two recounted what had taken place on the way and how he was made known to them in the breaking of the bread. (24:31-35)

For those disciples to say that their hearts were burning while Jesus spoke to them had to mean that they were over-joyed. Then, to discover the real presence of their Lord and Master when He broke the bread—what a celebration! How-ever, they did not have the chance to say anything to Jesus at that moment, for He vanished from their sight. And then, returning to Jerusalem after having made the long journey earlier that day back to their home—they surely must have wanted to celebrate and proclaim the appearance of Christ. This they did with the eleven apostles and the others who were with them.

****

A twenty-three year old man was tragically killed in a heli-copter crash. He left behind a young wife and two daughters. The wife came to me shortly after the funeral and was visibly angry. She approached me as a priest and spoke about how her pastor referred to the funeral of her deceased husband as a celebration. She quickly stated that losing her husband in such a tragic way was no reason to celebrate. She added that she not only despised the word "celebrate" but that she also had little respect for the priest who presided at the funeral Mass and spoke about the funeral as a celebration.

Quite often when we hear about a celebration we associate it with enjoyment over some event or some achievement. We celebrate milestones in a person's life or career. For example, we celebrate a person's sobriety over alcohol or when someone finds out that he or she is cancer-free. Children celebrate snow days which keep them from school and they celebrate the final day of school at the end of an academic year. Because the young wife whose husband was killed in a tragic accident had heard the word "celebration" associated with her husband's funeral, she felt that her husband's death was being treated disrespectfully.

As I listened to the young woman I felt sorry for her loss. I understood the hurt and even the bitterness that her words bespoke. I asked if she had any anger toward God, and her response indicated just the opposite. She accepted that the helicopter crash was the result of human error and, therefore, she did not blame God, nor did she hold any anger toward Him. She emphasized that her anger was toward the priest who referred to the funeral as a celebration. Because of the way that she responded to my question, I offered the following thought.

I told the young widow that I didn't know what her priest actually said or how he worded his comments about the funeral. I told her that perhaps the priest, when speaking about the funeral liturgy, might have been referring to the funeral *liturgy* as a celebration—specifically a celebration of our faith. In other words, the death of her husband was not a reason to celebrate—which is how she had interpreted the priest's words. I told her that despite the sadness of losing someone we love, for those who have the gift of faith and who believe in the promise of eternal life and of our own future resurrection, the liturgy of Christian burial offers for us the truth of what Jesus taught and can elicit from us a joyful hope in God's Providence.

****

Summary statement:

The Mass is a celebration of faith. When Mass begins, the priest exhorts the congregation with these words: "Brethren (brothers and sisters), let us acknowledge our sins, and so prepare ourselves to celebrate the sacred mysteries." The sacred mysteries will consist of hearing God's Word in Scripture and then entering into communion with Jesus and with one another. These sacred mysteries recall and celebrate the faith that we share in Jesus as our Lord.

Thus from celebration to celebration,
as they proclaim the Paschal mystery of Jesus
"until he comes," the pilgrim People of God advances,
following the narrow way of the cross,
toward the heavenly banquet, when all the elect
will be seated at the table of the kingdom.

Catechism of the Catholic Church, 1344

Cup of Blessing

I am speaking to sensible people; judge for yourselves what I am saying. The **cup** of blessing that we bless, is it not a participation in the blood of Christ? The bread that we break, is it not a participation in the body of Christ?

(1 Cor 10:15-16)

In the Gospel according to Mark we find Jesus heading toward Jerusalem with His disciples (Mk 10:32-45). The Gospel states that Jesus was ahead of the disciples who were amazed and afraid. They were amazed because Jesus was doing something that they had not expected. They were afraid because of what they could expect, knowing what awaited them in Jerusalem.

Going to Jerusalem was "code language" used by the Gospel writers to indicate that Jesus was preparing to accept His death and Resurrection that He had already foretold. He was telling His disciples that His was a life of service and He was preparing His disciples to realize that they, too, were called to this kind of service.

As the story continues, James and John catch up to Jesus, and knowing that they might also die in Jerusalem, they ask Jesus if they can be seated in glory with Him—one at His right and the other at His left. In one sense, these men were showing real courage by remaining with Jesus even though they knew their own lives were in jeopardy. On the other hand, they riled up the other disciples with the question they asked. Jesus responded to their question by asking, "Can you drink the cup that I drink or be baptized with the baptism with which I am baptized?" He then told them that it was up to His Father as to who would be at His right and left in the Kingdom. When the other disciples heard that James and John were asking for this favor, they were not too happy and began to throw barbs at James and John. Jesus used this as a teachable moment by reminding them that whoever wanted to be great among them should be willing to serve the needs of others.

"Drinking the cup" is a metaphor that is used in the Old Testament. It refers to a person accepting the destiny or the vocation that God has for them. For example, in Psalm 16:5 we read: "Lord, my allotted portion and my cup, you have made my destiny secure." The psalmist here may have been of the priestly class since he spoke of having the Lord as his cup and his heritage. In Jesus' case from the Gospel, the cup was God's divine judgment for His Son to take on sin in order to take away sin. In that sense, the cup from which we drink perhaps refers to our baptismal vocation which is to love Christ above all and to follow Him in the lifestyle to which He calls us.

When Jesus prayed in the Garden of Gethsemane on the night leading up to His death, He spoke to His Father with these words: "Father, if you are willing, take this cup away from me; still, not my will but yours be done" (Lk 22:42). These words reveal what was in the mind and heart of Jesus on that sorrowful night. Ultimately, even though Jesus knew that He would suffer, He was willing to submit completely to the will of God the Father. He knew that this was His vocation.

When I think about this I recall that Jesus is fully human and fully divine. In His human nature, He agonized when thinking about the torture and shame that He would endure. Nevertheless, He was willing to "drink the cup" in the sense that He was willing to accept the destiny that God the Father had for Him. Luke's Gospel indicates that "to strengthen him an angel from heaven appeared to him" (Lk 22:43) and that because of the agony He experienced, "his sweat became like drops of blood falling on the ground" (Lk 22:45).

The prayer of Jesus in the Garden shows us two important aspects of His submission to God the Father. He prays "if you are willing," thereby placing His ultimate trust in God's decision. He also prays "not my will but yours be done," indicating His submission to God's design for our redemption. The beautiful Letter to the Hebrews, referencing Christ's humanity and His submission to God's will, states the following:

> Therefore, he had to become like his brothers in every way, that he might be a merciful and faithful high priest before God to expiate the sins of the people. Because he himself was tested through what he suffered, he is able to help those who are being tested. (Heb 2:17-18)

The *cup* reference in Scripture that pertains directly to the Eucharist is found in Saint Paul's Letter to the Corinthians (1 Cor 10:15-16). When Paul wrote these words he was warning his fellow Christians not to fall into idolatry. The context surrounding Paul's words included his realization that just as the Christians offered sacrifice in their Eucharist, so did the pagans as well as the Jews who were not Christian. With each of these groups—Christian, pagan and Jewish—the sacrificial offerings established communion among themselves. Paul was stating here that communion with Christ was unique and wonderful, incompatible with the communion of any other group.

In another part of Saint Paul's Letter to the Corinthians he again treats of the institution of the Eucharist and the importance of worthy reception. He writes:

> Therefore whoever eats the bread or drinks the cup of the Lord unworthily will have to answer for the body and blood of the Lord. A person should examine himself, and so eat the bread and drink the cup. For anyone who eats and drinks without discerning the body, eats and drinks judgment on himself. (1 Cor. 11:27-29)

In the letter to the Corinthians Paul refers to the *cup of blessing*. The *Catechism of the Catholic Church* provides the following information about the cup of blessing:

> The "cup of blessing" at the end of the Jewish Passover meal adds to the festive joy of wine an eschatological dimension:

the messianic expectation of the rebuilding of Jerusalem. When Jesus instituted the Eucharist, he gave a new and definitive meaning to the blessing of the bread and the cup.[1]

Those who have studied the Passover ritual indicate that cups of wine are distributed and shared at four different times during the Passover meal.[2] Scripture scholars suggest that in the Gospel according to Luke, the reference to the *cup* that is found in Luke 22:17 refers to the *cup of blessing*. The cup of blessing, according to the Passover ritual, was the third of the four cups distributed and shared. We read the following in Luke's Gospel:

> Then he took a cup, gave thanks, and said, "Take this and share it among yourselves; for I tell you that from this time on I shall not drink of the fruit of the vine until the kingdom of God comes." Then he took the bread, said the blessing, broke it, and gave it to them, saying, "This is my body, which will be given for you; do this in memory of me." And likewise the cup after they had eaten, saying, "This cup is the new covenant in my blood, which will be shed for you." (Lk 22:17-20)

I will conclude this section with the following thought—in John's Gospel, as Jesus hung upon the Cross, He said, "I thirst" (Jn 19:28). Some "common wine" was available, and one of the soldiers put the wine on a sprig of hyssop and raised it to Jesus' mouth. "When Jesus had taken the wine, he said, 'It is finished.' And bowing his head, he handed over the spirit" (19:30). Interestingly, in Latin the phrase "It is finished" is translated as *Consummatum est*. What makes this interesting is that the fourth cup of the Passover meal is referred to as the "cup of consummation." If we recall, Jesus shared the "cup of blessing," the third cup, with His apostles at the Last Supper. However, as the Gospels according to Matthew and Mark

---

1   See *Catechism of the Catholic Church*, n. 1334.

2   One example of a biblical scholar who has studied the Passover and who describes the four cups shared at various times during the Passover meal is Dr. Scott Hahn, who gave a lecture entitled "The Fourth Cup." The CD (LH5-2) can be obtained through Lighthouse Catholic Media.

both indicate, Jesus mentioned that He would not drink the cup again, which seems to indicate that the Passover was not going to be completed on that night. We read in Matthew's Gospel:

> Then he took a cup, gave thanks, and gave it to them, saying, "Drink from it, all of you, for this is my blood of the covenant, which will be shed on behalf of many for the forgiveness of sins. I tell you, from now on I shall not drink this fruit of the vine until the day when I drink it with you anew in the kingdom of my Father." Then, after singing a hymn, they went out to the Mount of Olives. (Mt 26:27-30)

The "singing a hymn" most probably refers to Psalms 114-118 which would lead to the end of the Passover meal, the final act being to drink the fourth cup of wine. Do the Gospel accounts of the Last Supper suggest that Jesus did not drink the fourth cup? The Gospel according to Luke reminds us that Jesus shared a cup *after* the meal (Lk 22:19), and according to the ritual of the Passover, this would have been the third cup, the cup of blessing. Was the fourth cup, the cup of consummation, postponed? Was the fourth cup the "common wine" raised to the lips of Jesus on the Cross?[3] Recall also that after the Passover meal, Jesus and the apostles went to the Garden of Gethsemane where Jesus prayed, "My Father, if it is possible, let this cup pass from me; yet, not as I will, but as you will" (Mt 26:39). A second time that evening Jesus prayed, "My Father, if it is not possible that this cup pass without my drinking it, your will be done" (26:42).

I turn once again to the explanation given by Dr. Pitre, who writes the following:

> Given the Passover context of his prayer (it is still Passover night), and given the fact that he had just left the Upper Room, by now the answer seems clear: Jesus is praying to the Father about the fourth cup, the final cup of the Passover

---

3 In Dr. Hahn's lecture entitled "The Fourth Cup," he states that the fourth cup indeed was the cup of consummation given to Jesus as He hung upon the Cross. The final consummation, the wine that was given to Jesus as He died, brought about the new Passover—the new and eternal covenant.

liturgy. He has just celebrated the Last Supper, in which he identified his own *body* as the sacrifice of the new Passover. He has also just identified one of the cups of wine as his own *blood*, about to be poured out for the forgiveness of sins. In other words, Jesus implicitly identified himself as the new Passover lamb. The implication of this self-identification is sobering: by the time this new Passover is finished, Jesus will be dead. That's what happens to Passover lambs. They don't make it out alive.[4]

Dr. Pitre then suggests the following:

Therefore, Jesus not only celebrated the Jewish Passover that night in the Upper Room. As the long-awaited Messiah of Israel, the suffering servant who would give his life for "many" (Isaiah 53:10-12), Jesus also reconfigured the Passover around his own passion. By refusing to drink the fourth cup until his death on the Cross, he united the Last Supper to his own sacrificial death. And by commanding his disciples to repeat what he had done in the Upper Room, he deliberately perpetuated this new Passover—both sacrifice and meal—down through the ages.[5]

****

Patricia Polacco authored a short story called *The Blessing Cup*.[6] In it she tells the story of her great-grandmother, Anna, and Anna's life in Russia prior to and after being forced out of her country during World War II. Anna and her family, being Jewish, are forced out of Russia and they attempt to flee to America in order to find a better life. A family heirloom carries great importance in the story—a cup. A cherished tea set was given to Anna's great, great-grandmother when she married, and an accompanying note indicated that it was a magic tea set. The note further contained the message that those who drink from the tea set will never know a day of hunger and their lives will always have flavor. They will know love and joy and never experience poverty.

---

4   Pitre, 164.
5   Ibid., 173.
6   Patricia Polacco, *The Blessing Cup* (Simon and Schuster Books, 2013).

The story reveals, however, some of the horrible consequences of war and hatred. Anna and her family were driven from their homeland; her father became very ill, and they had to live hand-to-mouth for an extended period of time. The story, however, focused upon the blessings that they did receive. They arrived safely in America and they were cared for by a kind doctor who gave special attention to the ailing father in exchange for meals.

This is a story that moves the heart. It is about a cup, a man who cares for the poor and the ill, and about a meal with a family he has grown to love. Perhaps the story has some connection with our celebration of the Eucharist.

****

Summary statement:

One of the acclamations that can be spoken or sung after the Host and chalice are elevated at Mass recalls the cup of blessing. We say: "When we eat this Bread and drink this Cup, we proclaim your Death, O Lord, until you come again." The "Bread" and "cup" refer to the Real Presence of Christ that we adore and acknowledge in faith. It also represents our vocation to live with the attitude of Jesus. For us, it is truly the cup of blessing.

Take care, then, to have but one Eucharist. For there is one flesh of our Lord Jesus Christ, and one cup to show forth the unity of His blood; one altar, as there is one bishop, along with the priests and deacons, my fellow-servants.

St. Ignatius of Antioch, *Letters to the Philadelphians*

Covenant

> When Moses came to the people and related all the words
> and ordinances of the Lord, they all answered with one
> voice, "We will do everything that the Lord has told
> us." Moses then wrote down all the words of the Lord
> and, rising early in the morning, he built at the foot of
> the mountain an altar and twelve sacred stones for the
> twelve tribes of Israel. Then, having sent young men of
> the Israelites to offer burnt offerings and sacrifice young
> bulls as communion offerings to the Lord, Moses took half
> of the blood and put it in large bowls; the other half he
> splashed on the altar. Taking the book of the **covenant**,
> he read it aloud to the people, who answered,
> "All that the Lord has said, we will hear and do." Then he
> took the blood and splashed it on the people, saying,
> "This is the blood of the **covenant** which the Lord has
> made with you according to all these words."
>
> (Ex 24:3-8)

The Book of Genesis begins with a love story. God created
His crown jewel, the human person, because of His love. The
crown jewel received God's special favor by being created in
God's image and likeness. Further, the crown jewel entered
into a covenant with God whereby God offered His protection
for humankind. God's love was also the reason why He gave
the human person the gift of free will. However, free will gave
humans the capability to sin. Nevertheless, even in our sin,
God did not abandon us. There were consequences to sin and
to the breaking of the covenant—but God never abandoned us.

God's first covenant was with Adam. God knew that Adam
required a "suitable partner," so He provided. God gave Adam

and Eve free rein in the Garden of Eden except for the one pro-
hibition. They did not fight off the temptation, but succumbed
to sin. There were consequences to breaking the covenant, but
still, God did not abandon His crown jewel. As time passed,
sin gained a stronger foothold in the lives of humans. Sin led
to greater chaos and separation from God. The story involving
Noah and the flood is a reminder that the flood waters represented chaos and being cut off from the living God. Nevertheless, God continued His covenant with the crown jewel and
promised His continued protection.

The covenant that God made with Abraham stands out in
a striking way. Genesis 15 relates that covenant story. Actually, this covenant relationship begins in Genesis 12 when
God asked Abram (later his name was changed to Abraham)
to leave his home country and move to a land that God had in
mind. God initiated the covenant by saying to Abram:

> "I will make of you a great nation, and I will bless you; I
> will make your name great, so that you will be a blessing.
> I will bless those who bless you and curse those who curse
> you. All the families of the earth will find blessing in you."
> (Gen 12:2-3)

In the course of time when God and Abram were speaking,
Abram reminded God that he still did not have an heir. God
assured Abram that an heir would be given to him. Then, as
God showed Abram the land that lay before him, Abram asked
how he would come to possess it. God reassured Abram by
performing an ancient Near Eastern covenant ritual. According to this ritual, the covenanting parties would walk between
animals that had been killed, taking upon themselves the fate
of the animals should either party violate the covenant. God
instructed Abram to bring several animals to Him and, after-
ward, "a deep sleep fell upon Abram" (Gen 15:12).

The truly fascinating part of the story occurs when the *the-
ophany* (appearance of a deity) of God (i.e., a smoking fire pot
and a flaming torch) passes through the pieces of the animals

while Abram, the covenanting party, sleeps. In this God is holding Himself accountable to the covenant which He will not break and at the same time, frees humankind from the fate of eternal separation should the covenant be broken. What is all the more interesting in this story is that God who performs the covenant ritual is also the one who takes on the punishment when the covenant is broken. God does this when His Son accepts death on the Cross.

Other covenants in the Old Testament include those made with Moses and with King David. Finally, the greatest covenant of them all occurred. It was the new and eternal covenant given to us by the Son of God. The covenant with Jesus is the greatest of the covenants and shows us that God's protection continues to be upon us and will be with us until the end of time.

God's covenants are not static. They are not simply events of the past that have reached their completion. God communicated with humans by means of covenants time and again. The Old Testament stories of God's covenants show us some of the initial and varied ways by which God made covenants with humankind. As the Letter to the Hebrews indicates:

> In times past, God spoke in partial and various ways to our ancestors through the prophets; in these last days, he spoke to us through a son, whom he made heir of all things and through whom he created the universe, who is the refulgence of his glory, the very imprint of his being, and who sustains all things by his mighty word. (Heb 1:1-3a)

Between God and humankind, covenants are accompanied by signs, sacrifices, and solemn oaths that sealed the relationship with promises of blessing for keeping the covenant faithfully. In the Old Testament, also known as the Old Covenant, God revealed His love in a number of ways and offered protection and direction for His chosen people. In the New Testament, the New Covenant, God revealed through Christ a new and eternal covenant. This covenant was anticipated when Our Lord took bread and wine, elements of the Passover ritual, and

gave them new meaning during the Last Supper. This covenant was established with Christ's own sacrificial death and
Resurrection.

The Gospel according to Matthew places the word *covenant* on the lips of Jesus during the Last Supper when He said:
"Drink from it, all of you, for this is my blood of the covenant,
which will be shed on behalf of many for the forgiveness of
sins" (Mt 26:27-28). Saint Paul relates the same event of the
Last Supper in his Letter to the Corinthians when he writes:

> For I received from the Lord what I also handed on to you,
> namely that the Lord Jesus, on the night he was handed over,
> took bread, and, after he had given thanks, broke it and said,
> "This is my body that is for you. Do this in remembrance
> of me." In the same way also the cup, after supper, saying,
> "This cup is the new covenant in my blood. Do this, as often
> as you drink it, in remembrance of me." For as often as you
> eat this bread and drink this cup, you proclaim the death of
> the Lord until he comes. (1 Cor 11:23-26)

The words of Jesus over the cup of wine that Saint Paul
quoted, "This cup is the new covenant in my blood," are also
the words that Moses spoke when he ratified the Exodus covenant that God had made with His chosen people. In Exodus 24 we encounter Moses who erected an altar as God had
instructed. Moses placed twelve sacred stones around the altar
to represent the twelve tribes of Israel. Young bulls were then
chosen as the sacrificial offering to the Lord, and:

> Moses took half of the blood and put it in large bowls; the
> other half he splashed on the altar. Taking the book of the
> covenant[1] he read it aloud to the people, who answered,
> "All that the Lord has said, we will hear and do." The he
> took the blood and splashed it on the people, saying, "This

---

1   The "book of the covenant" mentioned in Ex 24:7 refers to the descriptive
laws that met the needs of the developing Israelite nation. These laws were ultimately based upon the Ten Commandments which God gave to the Israelites so
that they could live in accord with Him and with one another. The "book of the
covenant," while having its basis in the Ten Commandments, was a set of laws
given by Moses. Some of the laws were economic, some social and some spiritual.

is the blood of the covenant which the Lord has made with you according to all these words." (Ex 24:6-8)

Of all the words or phrases that speak to me about the Eucharist, the word *covenant* is most significant because it conveys the blessing that God continues to offer us in Christ and in His redemptive love. Each day when I offer the Holy Mass and pray the words of Jesus at the Last Supper, I realize that along with the angels and saints who surround me and all who are gathered to celebrate the Eucharist, I am really and truly in the presence of the Eternal Word. Therefore, in the Eucharist I find the solemn oath, the "pledge of future glory" spoken of in the text attributed to Saint Thomas Aquinas and honoring the Blessed Sacrament. The *Catechism of the Catholic Church* in paragraph 1405 makes reference to the "pledge of future glory," stating the following:

> There is no surer pledge or clearer sign of this great hope in the new heavens and new earth "in which righteousness dwells,"[2] than the Eucharist. Every time this mystery is celebrated, "the work of our redemption is carried on" and we "break the one bread that provides the medicine of immortality, the antidote for death, and the food that makes us live forever in Jesus Christ."[3]

****

A memory that I have as a young child is that of a picture on our living room wall. It was a painting of the face of Jesus. The portrait was painted by the American artist Warner Sallman in 1940. It gained greater notoriety in 1991 when a twelve-year-old boy who was battling leukemia and who was close to death regained his health. The boy and his family attribute his recovery to the Sallman portrait of Christ that was in their home.

Over many years I have kept a smaller version of the Sallman portrait of Christ in my breviary. I have often thought that one reason for my vocation to the priesthood might have been due to the attraction that the painting had over me even from my youth.

2   2 Pet 3:13.
3   *Lumen Gentium* 3: Saint Ignatius of Antioch, *Letter to the Ephesians*, 20.

On the morning of my fortieth anniversary of ordination to the priesthood, I received a gift from a dear friend. It was the Sallman portrait of Christ. My friend had no idea that it was this portrait that had inspired me years earlier. I told her how pleased I was to receive it and the significance that it holds for me. I still look at the Sallman painting and I think about the new and eternal covenant that is given to us by Christ who is really and sacramentally present in the Eucharist. The Eucharist is Christ's covenant of love for us.

****

Summary statement:

The new and eternal covenant that we receive in the Eucharist is a gift that communicates to us God's mercy. Without God's mercy none of us can be saved. With God's mercy we have received the fullness of redemption. It is Christ who has redeemed us and the Eucharist renews the pledge of God's mercy toward us.

We come up here against the real mark of the New Covenant: in Christ, God has bound Himself to men and has let Himself be bound by them. The New Covenant no longer rests on the reciprocal keeping of the agreement; it is granted by God as grace that abides even in the face of man's faithlessness. It is the expression of God's love, which will not be defeated by man's incapacity but always remains well disposed toward him, welcomes him again and again precisely because he is sinful, turns to him, sanctifies him, and loves him.

Father Joseph Ratzinger (later Pope Benedict XVI)
in *Introduction to Christianity*, p. 341

Christ

Now when they heard this, they were cut to the heart, and they asked Peter and the other apostles, "What are we to do, my brothers?" Peter [said] to them, "Repent and be baptized, every one of you, in the name of Jesus **Christ** for the forgiveness of your sins; and you will receive the gift of the holy Spirit.

(Acts 2:37-38)

From the Gospel according to Matthew we are told about a time when Jesus was with His disciples at Caesarea Philippi. He asked the disciples an interesting question, wondering how people perceived Him. They replied that some thought He was John the Baptist while others thought that perhaps He was Elijah having returned. Then He said to them, "But who do you say that I am?" to which Simon Peter responded, "You are the Messiah, the Son of the living God." (See Mt 16:15-17) The word *Messiah* is a Hebrew word which has as its Greek counterpart the word *Christ*. Both refer to the Anointed One of God. When we refer to Jesus as the Christ we are saying that He is God's Anointed One.

The setting for this Gospel scene is at Caesarea Philippi. We sometimes find significant information in what we might consider to be a minor detail. Here, for example, the detail of Jesus being with His disciples at Caesarea Philippi is perhaps minor but nevertheless significant.

There are several things that we can say about Caesarea Philippi at that time. First, it was considered the most pagan place in all of Palestine. Most devout Jews would avoid it completely, yet Jesus went there deliberately. Secondly, the city was built on top of rock—some estimates indicating that it was one hundred feet of solid rock straight up. Thirdly, the city's pagan influence was due to the fact that it was the center of worship to the god Pan, the pagan god of nature and fertility, and where a temple had been erected in his honor. Being a god of fertility, followers of Pan would honor his festivals by performing lewd and distasteful acts, including prostitution and sexual interaction between humans and goats since Pan was half human and half goat. Finally, next to Pan's temple was a great crevice in the ground that was thought to be the place where the dead spirits would go to and from Hades, the underworld. It was called "the Gates of Hell" or the "Gates of Hades."   •

In summary, Caesarea Philippi was a city built on a solid rock foundation. It was a city of moral darkness and sin. It was also a location where people believed that the underworld with its evil spirits had some power over them.

Jesus went there deliberately, and going into that region He asked His disciples who people say that He is. Recall that this is where Pan was considered to be a god. After hearing the disciples' responses, Jesus asked who *they* thought He was. Simon Peter's answer must have pleased Jesus, so in the city built on rock, Jesus tells Simon Peter, "You are Peter, and upon this rock I will build my church, and the gates of the netherworld shall not prevail against it" (Mt 16:18). In that moment, Jesus changed Simon's name to *Peter,* the Latin derivative for the word "rock." Just as Caesarea Philippi was built on a rock foundation, Jesus was going to build His Church on a solid foundation—and Simon would be the rock with the authority to lead.

In that minor detail of locating this conversation at Caesarea Philippi we find 1) a new foundation for His Church; 2) a new light where Jesus went deliberately into a place of moral darkness; and 3) a word to His disciples that the Gates of Hades (Hell) will not prevail against His Kingdom. Yes, there may be and there are attacks against His Church—both from within and without—but no evil force will ever prevail against His Church.

How might we apply this to ourselves as we consider the gift of the Eucharist? First, we have the Church as our foundation. We can be grateful for the presence of Christ as Founder and for the Sacraments and the Tradition that has been given to us through Christ. Secondly, at Caesarea Philippi Jesus revealed the glory of Who He is in perhaps the darkest corner of Palestine. The Church is called to enter into some of the dark moral corners of the world—and personally, Christ comes into the dark corners of our own lives and waits for us to accept His forgiving love. Thirdly, although the Church may face difficulties, persecution, etc., the powers of evil will not prevail over the Church that has been founded by the Anointed One, the Christ.

Jesus said that no evil force would ever prevail against His Church. The Eucharist, for the Church, might be called the medicine of immortality, given to us until the end of time when Christ returns in glory. Saint Ignatius of Antioch referred to the Eucharist in those terms in the conclusion of his Letter to the Ephesians written before 110 A.D. These are his words about Christ and the Eucharist, the medicine of immortality:

> If Jesus Christ shall graciously permit me through your prayers, and if it be His will, I shall, in a second little work which I will write to you, make further manifest to you the nature of the dispensation of which I have begun to treat, with respect to the new man, Jesus Christ, in His faith and in His love, in His suffering and in His resurrection.

> Especially will I do this if the Lord make known to me that you come together in common, man by man, through grace—individually, in one faith, and in Jesus Christ, who was of the seed of David according to the flesh, being both the Son of man and the Son of God;

> And if you thus obey the bishop and the presbytery with an undivided mind, breaking one and the same bread, which is

the medicine of immortality, and the antidote to prevent us from dying, but which causes that we should live forever in Jesus Christ.[4]

****

The Roman sky was a brilliant blue that day with perhaps two or three clouds wafting overhead in that perfect scene. It was the first time I had been to the Vatican. I stood before the magnificent obelisk and read the inscription: *Christus vincit—Christus regnat—Christus imperat; Christus ab omni malo plebem suam defendat.* The English translation would read: Christ conquers—Christ reigns—Christ commands; may Christ defend His people from all evil.

The four verbs contained in the inscription are in the present tense. This serves as a reminder that Christ's triumph over sin and death is not a past event. His triumph continues today and throughout all eternity. In His real and sacramental presence among us, Christ continues to conquer sin, to reign as King of the Universe, to command us in the way of love and to defend us from the powers of evil.

****

Summary statement:

In the region of Caesarea Philippi, a city known for its pagan temples to Zeus and Pan, Jesus asked His disciples this question about Himself: "Who do you say that I am?" Simon Peter replied, "You are the Christ, the Son of the Living God" (Mt 16:16). He knew that Jesus was the Anointed One, the Messiah of God. Jesus acknowledged Peter's response with a gift for us all—the gift of Christ's abiding presence in the Church that He founded.

---

4   Saint Ignatius of Antioch, *Letter to the Ephesians*, n. 20.

The more we come to know and love our Eucharistic Lord,
the more we understand our mission of bringing our Lord
to the world. As Pope Benedict XVI reminds us, we do not
offer to the world "just a theory of a way of life inspired by
Christ, but the gift of his very person"

(Sacramentum Caritatis, 86).

Today there is a strong tendency to make our witness
acceptable to a world which is marked by a great diversity
of peoples and beliefs. The Holy Eucharist reminds us that
our testimony must be a clear witness to the person of our
Lord Jesus Christ and the salvation which He alone brings
to the world. In other words, our witness must be a sound
and uncompromising proclamation of the truth about our
Lord Jesus Christ.

Raymond Cardinal Burke, *Divine Love Made Flesh*, 180

A B C

Once more we'll try an ABC:
From Greek and Hebrew these words will be.

****

Anamnesis – Berakah – Crisis

****

Anamnesis

For I received from the Lord what I also handed on to you: that the Lord Jesus, on the night he was handed over, took bread, and, after he had given thanks, broke it and said, "This is my body that is for you. Do this in **remembrance** of me." In the same way also the cup, after supper, saying, "This cup is the new covenant in my blood. Do this, as often as you drink it, in **remembrance** of me." For as often as you eat this bread and drink the cup, you proclaim the death of the Lord until he comes.

(1 Cor 11:23-26)

The first off-Broadway musical that I ever saw was *The Fantasticks*. The plot developed around two fathers, in fact two neighbors, who trick their children into falling in love by pretending to have a family feud. After these many years I cannot remember too much about the play except for the song *Try to Remember* which helped to transition from the opening of the play to its final curtain.

Try to remember—that is what the word *anamnesis* means. *Anamnesis* is the Greek word that means *memory*. That's the beauty of *anamnesis*—in which the memory relives and makes present what occurred in the past. Father Cantamalessa suggests the following to help illustrate the point:

> History reveals what happened once and how it happened, the liturgy keeps the past from being forgotten; not in the sense that it makes the past event happen again (*non faciendo*), but in the sense that it celebrates it (*sed celebrando*).... The Mass renews the event of the Cross by celebrating it (not by reiterating it!) and celebrates it by renewing it (not just by recalling it!). The word that meets with

the greatest ecumenical consent today is, perhaps, the verb *represent* (also used by Paul VI in his encyclical *Mysterium fidei*), understood in its strongest sense, re-present or, make present again.[1]

Bishop Fulton J. Sheen offered a similar thought when he wrote:

> Calvary took up only a moment of time, but being the sacrifice of the Eternal God made man, it was capable of illumining the whole of time in all periods of history. The Mass is the projection in time of the eternal values of Calvary. ... The Mass is not a *new sacrifice* but another *enactment* of the one supreme sacrifice of Calvary.[2]

As a priest, when I lift the Host at the consecration of the Mass, I pray silently, "My Lord and my God," the words that Thomas said as he saw Jesus for the first time after Christ's Resurrection (see Jn 20:28). After that I also say silently, "Behold, God's love for you" before lowering the Host and placing it once again upon the altar. Then, taking the chalice and elevating it, I say "My Jesus, mercy," for me a reminder that Jesus' blood is the merciful gift of redemption that we have all received. Immediately after that I say quietly, "Bring this to life again."

The two phrases, "Behold, God's love for you" and "Bring this to life again" require a bit of explanation. The first, "Behold, God's love for you" helps me to recall the *Bread of the Presence* (sometimes referred to as the "showbread") that the Lord had instructed Moses to prepare so that proper worship could be given to God. The central place of worship was to be in the location of the Tabernacle where two significant items, the Ark of the Covenant as well as the Bread of the Presence, were to be kept. The instruction from the Lord to Moses with regard to the Bread of the Presence is clear: "On the table you shall always keep showbread set before me" (Ex 25:30). Although

---

1   Cantalamessa, 12-13.
2   Bishop Fulton J. Sheen wrote the Introduction to *This is the Mass*, published by Hawthorn Books, Inc. in 1958. This quote is found on pages 10-11.

called the Bread of the Presence, the instruction from the Lord also mandated that on the table "You shall make its plates and cups, as well as its pitchers and bowls for pouring libations" (Ex 25:29), suggesting that both bread and wine were to be a part of the sacrificial offering to God. The Bread of the Presence, commanded by God to be shown and offered in worship, was seen as the visible sign of God's abiding presence. Even more, it was seen as a visible sign of God's covenant between Himself and the twelve tribes of Israel.

In the Book of Leviticus we find the following:

> You shall take bran flour and bake it into twelve cakes, using two tenths of an ephah of flour for each cake. These you shall place in two piles, six in each pile, on the pure gold table before the Lord. With each pile put some pure frankincense, which shall serve as an oblation to the Lord, a token of the bread offering. Regularly on each Sabbath day the bread shall be set out before the Lord on behalf of the Israelites by an everlasting covenant. It shall belong to Aaron and his sons, who must eat it in a sacred place, since it is most sacred. (Lev 24:5-9)

The text mentions that this Bread of the Presence was to be a visible sign of God's everlasting covenant. The twelve cakes signified that the covenant was made with the twelve tribes of Israel. Additionally, the use of pure frankincense meant that this was to be a sacrificial offering since incense rising to heaven was used with such offerings. We also read that the showbread was to be set before the Lord each Sabbath. Dr. Pitre offers the following:

> In the Tabernacle (and, later, the Jerusalem Temple), the Sabbath was distinctively marked by priestly sacrifices, both bloody and unbloody. Significantly, the unbloody sacrifice offered each week was nothing other than the Bread and wine of the Presence. It was only after the Romans destroyed the Temple in A.D. 70 that the offering of all sacrifices ceased. Before that tragic event, every week, Sabbath worship revolved around the offering of the fresh Bread of

the Presence and of the eating of the bread by the priests in the Holy Place.[3]

The Bread of the Presence was kept in the Temple in Jesus' time. Traditionally there were three times each year when Jewish men living in Israel would go to the Temple (see Ex 34:23). During these times the priests of the Temple would bring the table out from the Holy of Holies so that the pilgrims who were at the Temple in Jerusalem could see the Bread of the Presence. The priests would elevate the bread, saying "Behold, God's love for you!"[4]

The Bread of the Presence, the showbread, connects intimately with our gift of the Eucharist. The Bread of the Presence was a covenant. It was also a sacred bond renewed each Sabbath, and a sacrificial offering. For us, the Eucharist has become the new and eternal covenant, a sacred bond renewed each time the Holy Mass is offered, and a sacrificial offering where Jesus is both the priest and the victim. Jesus, in His real and sacramental presence in the Eucharist, is God's love for us in all of its profundity. I think of this each time when I hold the consecrated bread during the elevation at the Mass. When I pray silently, "Behold, God's love for you," I recall what the priests of the Old Testament said when holding the Bread of the Presence for all to see.

The second phrase, "Bring this back to life again" more closely connects with the Greek language. In English we say "Do this in memory of me," but this is where memory (*anamnesis*) can be confusing.

The concept of *anamnesis* may be one of the most difficult of concepts to grasp. We often think of past events and hold them in memory. There is something "more" when we consider a past event and re-present it or re-actualize it. Our Jewish sisters and brothers have an understanding of *anamnesis* in

---

3   Pitre, 124-125.
4   A thorough explanation of the Bread of the Presence can be found in Dr. Pitre's book, *Jesus and the Jewish Roots of the Eucharist*, 118-134.

their annual Seder meal at Passover time. During the Seder, a child asks, "Why is this night different from all other nights?" When the answer is given, there is a retelling of the story of how God freed the Israelites from the slavery that they had endured in Egypt. When the story is retold, it is meant to re-create or re-present what occurred in the past. The deeds of God that occurred in the past are retold in such a way that they become present once again for those celebrating the Seder ritual. Similar to the Passover meal that Jesus and His apostles memorialized at the Last Supper, the Eucharist is meant to be for us the memorial, the *anamnesis*, the ever-present sacrifice of Christ that was offered once and for all.

When the chalice is elevated during the Holy Mass and the priest says "Do this in memory of me," it is not merely an opportunity for us to recall what Jesus did two thousand years ago. We are asked to bring the Calvary event of the past to life again but not in the bloody manner in which Jesus died upon the Cross. The sacrificial offering of Jesus, although offered in an unbloody manner upon the altar in distinction from the bloody offering at Calvary, is nevertheless re-presented so that we are given the effects of Jesus' life, death, Resurrection and Ascension in the *here and now*. In other words, we are participants in the Eucharistic mystery and not simply onlookers. The *anamnesis* is the central part of the liturgy, reminding us that Christ's sacrifice enters into our space and time and takes place in the here and now.

In paragraph 1363 of the *Catechism of the Catholic Church* we read:

> In the sense of Sacred Scripture *the memorial is not merely the recollection of past events* but the proclamation of the mighty works wrought by God for men. In the liturgical celebration of these events, *they become in a certain way present and real.* This is how Israel understands its liberation from Egypt: every time Passover is celebrated, the Exodus events are made present to the memory of believers so that they may conform their lives to them.

Focusing again upon the Seder meal, it is important to recall that the roasted lamb was the item that Moses told the Israelites they were to eat (see Ex 12:8-12). On the Passover night the ritual prescribed by Moses was not completed simply by killing the lamb and sprinkling its blood on the doorposts; rather, the flesh of the sacrificial lamb was to be eaten. Moses also told the Israelites that the Passover was to be "a day of remembrance" (12:14), an *anamnesis*.

With that in mind, every Seder meal re-presents what occurred at the first Passover—that is, a sacrificial meal. It is for this reason that we speak of the Mass as the *Holy Sacrifice of the Mass*. The "sacrifice" of Christ is renewed; it is re-presented, albeit in an unbloody manner. It is because of the *anamnesis* that the sacrifice of Calvary is brought back to life during the Eucharistic Prayer of the Mass. Therefore, once again, although the concept of *anamnesis* is perhaps somewhat difficult to fully grasp, it is, nevertheless, essential for our understanding of the Eucharist and the real presence of Christ in the sacrament.

It is a difficult concept to wrap our minds around: the fact that the Mass is the sacrifice of Christ renewed. How can that be since, as the Letter to the Hebrews (9:28) states, Christ died once and for all? If Christ died once, then how can we say that the sacrifice of Christ is renewed? The answer is that Christ, now glorified, dies no more. However, He is still able to offer Himself in sacrifice. How so? The reason is because Christ is glorified in His humanity and in His divinity. In His humanity Christ is really present on the altar. With His human will Christ continues to surrender Himself to the Father as He intercedes for us. He does not die again on the altar; however, His self-surrender takes place, because Christ who is really present on the altar makes that sacrifice on our behalf. Thus, the sacrifice of Calvary is renewed. It is not the bloody sacrifice that took place once and for all on Calvary; rather, it is the unbloody sacrifice that occurs at every Mass. This concept was defined at the Council of Trent in the sixteenth century and was reiterated in the Second Vatican Council document, *Sacrosanctum concilium*, which addressed this aspect. In paragraph 47 we read about the "sacrifice" of Christ that is renewed each time the sacred liturgy is celebrated:

> Our Savior inaugurated the Eucharistic sacrifice of his body and blood at the Last Supper on the night he was betrayed, *in order to make his sacrifice of the cross last throughout time until he should return*; and indeed to entrust a token to the Church, his beloved wife, *by which to remember his death and resurrection*. It is a sacrament of faithful relationships, a sign of unity, a bond of divine love, a special Easter meal. In it, "Christ is received, the inner self is filled with grace, and a pledge of future glory is given to us."[1]

The Gospel according to John reminds us that when Jesus hung upon the Cross, He said, "I thirst" (Jn 19:28). We can imagine that for about eighteen hours Jesus would have had nothing to drink—nothing while in the Garden of Olives, nothing while interrogated by Pilate and others, nothing while being scourged and then mocked with a crown of thorns, and nothing while carrying the cross beam on His way to the place of crucifixion.

In addition to Jesus' physical thirst, we can also consider how Jesus—God Himself—was thirsting for us to be reconciled to Him. God's abiding love was poignantly revealed, since it was God who initiated the reconciliation by giving us His only-begotten Son so that we might not perish but might have eternal life (see Jn 3:16). The sacrifice of Jesus on the Cross was a bloody sacrifice. It was a self-offering that was made with love; Jesus in His human nature surrendered His will to the will of the Father.

God continues to thirst for us and desires that we be reconciled to Him. This will be a constant until the end of time. God, who thirsts for us, continues to reconcile us to Himself. However, Christ died once and for all. Nevertheless, Christ

---

1 Vatican Council II, Constitution *Sacrosanctum concilium,* "On the Sacred Liturgy," n. 47, p. 830.

continues to make a self-offering, a self-surrender to the Father's will. This is what occurs at each Mass, and when we receive the Body and Blood of the Lord in the Eucharistic sacrifice, we receive Christ in the fullness of His glorified divinity and humanity.

The Second Vatican Council, in *Lumen gentium*, spoke not only of Christ's self-offering but also of that of the Blessed Mother. Her role in Christ's sacrifice is stated in the following:

> This motherhood of Mary in the economy of grace goes on without interruption from the consent she faithfully gave at the Annunciation, which she upheld without wavering at the foot of the cross, right on to the perpetual consummation of all the elect. For assumed into heaven she has not put aside this saving role, rather she continues by her many prayers of intercession to obtain for us gifts of eternal salvation. In her motherly love she looks after the sisters and brothers of her Son who are still on their pilgrimage and placed amidst dangers and difficulties, until they are led to their happy homeland. Therefore in the Church the blessed Virgin is invoked by the titles of advocate, benefactress, helper and mediatrix. This, however, must be understood in such a way that it takes away nothing from the dignity and power of Christ the one mediator, and adds nothing on to this. For no creatures can ever be counted along with the incarnate Word and redeemer; but just as the priesthood of Christ is shared in a variety of ways both by ministers and by the faithful people, and just as the one goodness of God is really poured out on creatures in diverse ways, so also the one mediation of the redeemer does not rule out, but rouses up among creatures, participated cooperation from the one unique source.[2]

In the aforementioned paragraph 1363 from the *Catechism of the Catholic Church* we read that the Scriptural and liturgical understanding of *memorial* is not simply the recollection of a past event (e.g., Christ's death on the Cross) but also a proclamation of what God has wrought by that event as well

---

2   Vatican Council II, Dogmatic Constitution *Lumen gentium*, "On the Church," n. 62, pp. 895-896.

as the saving effects that continue in the present. A college student asked me about the distinction between the bloody sacrifice of Christ at Calvary and the unbloody sacrifice that occurs during the Mass. He said, "Okay, so if Christ doesn't die during the Mass, then why do we still call it the *sacrifice of the Mass*?" He asked a good question, and I believe that the answer lies in the way that we perceive the word *sacrifice*. A sacrifice is a self-offering that is made because of love. Jesus' sacrifice at Calvary was His self-surrender to the Father's will by accepting death on the Cross. Christ died once and for all. However, Christ continues to intercede for us at the right hand of the Father. This is His continued sacrifice, His self-offering that He makes because of His love for us.

In the preface (see Preface III for Easter) of the Easter season we are given the distinction between Christ's sacrifice at Calvary and His ongoing sacrifice that occurs on the altar. The sacrifice at Calvary is where "He is the sacrificial Victim who dies no more, the Lamb once slain." The sacrifice of the Mass is where "he never ceases to offer himself for us but defends us and ever pleads our cause" before God the Father. Simply stated, in the Eucharist Christ's sacrifice is not merely a historical memory; He is a present reality.

The following charts are an attempt to show the similarities and differences between the bloody sacrifice of Calvary and the unbloody sacrifice of the Mass.

The Sacrifice of Calvary	*The Sacrifice of the Mass*
Meaning of "sacrifice": Self-offering made by Jesus out of love	*Meaning of "sacrifice":* Continued self-offering by Jesus out of love
Context of the sacrifice being offered: Self-surrender to the Father's will	*Context of the sacrifice being offered:* Continued self-surrender to the Father's will

Purpose of the sacrifice:
Redemption obtained by
Jesus *once and for all*

Type of sacrifice:
Bloody—the physical body
of Jesus actually dying on
the Cross

*The difference between
Calvary and the Mass:*
Christ died because He
accepted what the Father
had asked of Him on our
behalf.

Purpose of the sacrifice:
Ongoing redemption for the
Father's children

Type of sacrifice:
Unbloody—Christ does
not die physically but He
surrenders His will to the
Father

*The difference between
Calvary and the Mass:*
Christ dies no more—but
continues to surrender to the
Father's will and to intercede
for us.

*Example of the bloody
sacrifice from Preface III
of Easter:*

He never ceases to offer
himself for us but defends
us and ever pleads our
cause before you: *He is the
sacrificial Victim who dies
no more, the Lamb, once
slain,* who lives forever.

*Example of the unbloody
sacrifice from Preface III
of Easter:*

*He never ceases to offer
himself for us but defends
us and ever pleads our
cause before you:* He is the
sacrificial Victim who dies
no more, the Lamb, once
slain, who lives forever.

Occasionally Judge Judy Scheindlin, in her nationally-syn-
dicated reality courtroom series, adjudicates cases involving
car mishaps. A rendering of the accident is drawn on a chart
and both the plaintiff and the defendant have the opportunity
to approach the chart and provide their recollection of the

mishap. In so doing, each party calls to mind what he or she remembers of the situation. With oral description of what happened as well as with photographs of the damaged vehicle, the plaintiff not only remembers the accident but re-presents the details so that Judge Judy can render an adequate decision and bring resolution to the case.

After the consecration during the Mass, the prayer of remembrance whereby the Church calls to mind Christ's Paschal Mystery is referred to as the *anamnesis*. The etymology of the Greek word αναμνεσις pertains to something being called to mind. Thus, the Church calls to mind and re-presents the one, all-sufficient, bloody sacrifice of Jesus at Calvary. The sacrifice of Calvary is made present in an unbloody manner on the altar where the bread and wine are transformed into the body and blood of our Lord. Jesus is not re-sacrificed at each Mass. However, each Mass re-presents the one sacrifice that occurred at Calvary.

At the Last Supper when Jesus offered the bread and the wine, stating that it was His body and blood, He was making the future sacrifice at Calvary present to His apostles. Then He told the apostles to repeat this in memory of Him.

When we participate in the Mass we hear the priest proclaim the words of Jesus when He says, "Do this in remembrance of me." The English is less accurate than the Greek in which the words of Jesus more correctly say, "Bring this [covenant] back to life again." To bring the covenant back to life again means that we are not simply remembering what Christ did in the past; we re-present at that moment, in an unbloody manner, what Jesus did when He suffered and died. In this way, the Last Supper makes the sacrifice of Calvary present once again, and this mystery will continue during each Mass until the Lord's return at the end of time. The *anamnesis* truly is a mystery—one which presents Christ's once-and-for-all sacrifice and brings that covenant to life again. The priest, obeying Christ's command, invokes the Holy Spirit who changes bread and wine into the body and blood of Christ, thereby bringing Christ's presence to the faithful.

****

Summary statement:

In the liturgy we participate in the mysteries and the events that brought about our salvation. This, however, is not simply a commemoration of past events. In the liturgy Christ is present through the power of the Holy Spirit, and the saving events become real in the here-and-now.

It may be said that at the Last Supper the cross of Christ
and the Christian Eucharist have inseparably received
a sacrificial character from Jesus,—the cross of Christ
because he handed himself over to it at the Last Supper as
an immolated oblation, like that of the Passover lamb, in
order to effect the new and eternal covenant conforming
to the divine plan "acknowledged" in his Eucharist,—
the Christian Eucharist, because it becomes at the same
moment the "memorial" of Jesus and of his salvific act.
Every time Christians celebrate it, as St. Paul says, they
"announce" or "proclaim" this death, not first to the world
but to God, and the "recalling" of Christ's death is for God
the pledge of his fidelity in saving them.

Louis Bouyer
Eucharist: Theology and Spirituality of the Eucharistic Prayer, 105

Berakoth

Blessed are you, Lord God of all creation,
for through your goodness we have received
the bread we offer you:
fruit of the earth and work of human hands,
it will become for us the bread of life.
Blessed be God forever.

Blessed are you, Lord God of all creation,
for through your goodness
we have received the wine we offer you:
fruit of the vine and work of human hands,
it will become our spiritual drink.
Blessed be God forever.

(From the Offertory of the Mass)

Every Catholic who faithfully participates in the Mass realizes that the aforementioned words are taken from the Preparation of the Gifts of bread and wine. This is a Hebrew *berakah* (plural, *berakoth*.) In Judaism, various *berakoth* or expressions of praise and thanks directed to God are offered at various times of the day. The *berakoth* are offered during synagogue services as well as at home in private prayer, for example when saying a prayer of blessing before a meal.[1] Psalm 104, for example, begins with a blessing of God for His goodness. The Psalm begins: "Bless the Lord, my soul! Lord, my God, you are great indeed!" The Psalm continues by singing the praises of God for the ways in which He reveals Himself to us.

---

1 A well-developed explanation of the *berakah* can be found in the work of Johannes H. Emminghaus, *The Eucharist: Essence, Form, Celebration* (Liturgical Press: Collegeville, 1997) 23-27.

Father Louis Bouyer, in his well-documented study of the development of the Christian Eucharist, explains how the Eucharistic rite of the liturgy had its origins in the Jewish meal prayers, the *berakoth*. He mentions in his book how the *berakoth* "contribute to making the whole life of the pious Jew an unceasingly renewed act of awareness of God in all things, and of his Word in all human actions."[2] The classic form of the *berakah* consists of the following: "Blessed (art) thou, Adonai, our God, king of the ages (or 'of the universe')."[3] As Father Bouyer points out, the name *Adonai* was the divine name that had been revealed to Moses on Mount Horeb when God appeared out of the burning bush (see Ex 3:1-4:23). When the *berakah* is offered with sincerity, it is offered to God "as the hidden King of all things, the one who holds the ages in his hand by his almighty Wisdom: the Master of the world throughout all of its history."[4]

In Saint Paul's Letter to Timothy we can find a reference to the *berakah*. One of Paul's themes is that the transmission of the truth affirms that Jesus is the Mediator of our redemption and that when we accept this truth, the pathway to our salvation has begun. Paul writes: "For everything created by God is good and nothing is to be rejected when received with thanksgiving, for it is made holy by the invocation of God in prayer" (1 Tim 4:4-5). When Paul mentioned "the invocation of God in prayer" he was referring here to the name of God being invoked in blessing (*berakah*).

In *Sacramentum Caritatis*, Pope Benedict XVI also mentions the *berakah*. He writes:

> This leads us to reflect on the institution of the Eucharist at the Last Supper. It took place within a ritual meal commemorating the foundational event of the people of Israel: their deliverance from slavery in Egypt. This ritual meal,

---

2   Louis Bouyer of the Oratory, *Eucharist: Theology and Spirituality of the Eucharistic Prayer* (University of Notre Dame Press: South Bend, 1968), 55.

3   Ibid, 56.

4   Ibid, 56.

which called for the sacrifice of lambs (cf. Ex 12:1-28, 43-51), was a remembrance of the past, but at the same time a prophetic remembrance, the proclamation of a deliverance yet to come. The people had come to realize that their earlier liberation was not definitive, for their history continued to be marked by slavery and sin. The remembrance of their ancient liberation thus expanded to the invocation and expectation of a yet more profound, radical, universal and definitive salvation. This is the context in which Jesus introduces the newness of His gift. In the prayer of praise, the *Berakah*, he does not simply thank the Father for the great events of past history, but also for his own "exaltation." In instituting the sacrament of the Eucharist, Jesus anticipates and makes present the sacrifice of the Cross and the victory of the resurrection. At the same time, he reveals that he himself is the true sacrificial lamb, destined in the Father's plan from the foundation of the world, as we read in the First Letter of Peter (cf. 1:18-20). By placing his gift in this context, Jesus shows the salvific meaning of his death and resurrection, a mystery which renews history and the whole cosmos. The institution of the Eucharist demonstrates how Jesus' death, for all its violence and absurdity, became in him a supreme act of love and mankind's definitive deliverance from evil.[5]

The goal of the *berakah* is to praise God for the blessings that He has bestowed upon us. It is an expression of glorifying God. In a sense, when we pray the Gloria at Mass, we are offering a *berakah* with these words: "We praise you. We bless you. We adore you. We glorify you. We give you thanks for your great glory, Lord God, heavenly King; O God, Almighty Father." Father Bouyer reminds us:

> The constant practice of the *berakoth* actually becomes an all-embracing prayer, involving the life of man and the world, whereby all things are brought back to the creative Word and restored to the original goodness which it had conferred upon them. As the Rabbis again tell us, this is how the whole faithful life of the people of Israel, even in

---

5 *Sacramentum Caritatis*, n. 10.

its apparently most mundane occupations, is clothed with a character that is not only sacred by also priestly. There are thereby that priest-people spoken of in the book of Exodus, because their whole life, taken in the framework of the *berakoth*, re-consecrates the entire universe to its author through the Word of God and prayer.[6]

****

About a year ago I spoke with a couple who were preparing for marriage. The young woman was Catholic, and her husband-to-be was Jewish. They were planning to marry out of state closer to his relatives and to have their marriage witnessed by a rabbi who was a relative of the man's family. The woman asked if the Catholic Church had any prayers of blessing that were offered during a wedding when a Catholic marries. The young couple told me about the seven blessings (*berakoth*) that are a key part of a traditional Jewish wedding ceremony. The seven blessings are adapted from rabbinic instructions that begin with a blessing over food and drink and conclude with a blessing that gives thanks to God for the joy of a fruitful marriage. The young man said that the blessing also included the praise of God, for He is ultimately the cause for rejoicing on the wedding day. As I listened, I realized that the prayers were indeed in praise of God who has made woman and man into His image and likeness.

I asked the young woman if she had ever listened to the Nuptial Blessing that is offered during the wedding ceremony in the Catholic Church. She said that although she had been to many Catholic weddings, she could not remember any special blessing for the newly-married couple. In the Catholic *Order of Celebrating Matrimony*[7] the Nuptial Blessing is given. I asked the young couple to read the blessing. They both loved it—especially with references to the Old Testament. The blessing is replete with what could be called *berakoth*:

---

6   Bouyer, 58.
7   USCCB, *The Order of Celebrating Matrimony* (Catholic Book Publishing Corp.: New Jersey, 2016), 36-37.

O God, who by your mighty power created all things out of nothing, and, when you had set in place the beginnings of the universe, formed man and woman in your own image, making the woman an inseparable helpmate to the man, that they might no longer be two, but one flesh, and taught that what you were pleased to make one must never be divided;

O God, who consecrated the bond of Marriage by so great a mystery that in the wedding covenant you foreshadowed the Sacrament of Christ and His Church;

O God, by whom woman is joined to man and the companionship they had in the beginning of creation is endowed with the one blessing not forfeited by original sin nor washed away by the flood;

Look now with favor on these your servants, joined together in Marriage, who ask to be strengthened by your blessing. Send down on them the grace of the Holy Spirit and pour your love into their hearts, that they may remain faithful in the Marriage covenant.

May the grace of love and peace abide in your daughter N., and let her always follow the example of those holy women whose praises are sung in the Scriptures.

May her husband entrust his heart to her, so that, acknowledging her as his equal and his joint heir to the life of grace, he may show her due honor and cherish her always with the love that Christ has for his Church.

And now, Lord, we implore you: may these your servants hold fast to the faith and keep your commandments; made one in the flesh, may they be blameless in all they do; and with the strength that comes from the Gospel, may they bear true witness to Christ before all; (may they be blessed with children, and prove themselves virtuous parents, who live to see their children's children).

And grant that, reaching at last together the fullness of years for which they hope, they may come to the life of the blessed in the Kingdom of Heaven. We ask this through Christ our Lord. Amen.

Summary statement:

Psalm 103 is but one example of blessing the Lord for His many blessings in our lives. It is an example of the *berakah*. "Bless the Lord, O my soul, and all my being, bless His holy name. Bless the Lord, O my soul, and forget not all His benefits."

Saint Polycarp of Smyrna was martyred in the latter half of the second century. According to the *Martyrdom of Polycarp*, a writing that contains the story the persecution and martyrdom of the saint, he was burned at the stake but then stabbed when the fire failed to harm him. In his words, he shows that he is going to his martyrdom with the same praise that he would have if he were to be celebrating the Eucharist for the last time. His prayer "espouses the whole development of the Jewish *berakah*: praise of the creator, then of the redeemer, the presentation of the 'memorial' with the supplication that the offering be accepted, and the final doxology."[8] The following prayer is attributed to Polycarp:

> Lord, Almighty God, Father of Jesus Christ,
> thy beloved and blessed child, through whom we have
> known thee, God of the Angels and the powers,
> God of all creation and of the whole family of the
> righteous who live in thy presence: I blessed thee for
> having judged me worthy of this day and this hour,
> for being counted among the number of thy martyrs
> and for sharing the cup of thy Christ, that I may rise
> to the everlasting life of the soul and the body in the
> incorruptibility of the Holy Spirit.

May I today, together with them, be received into thy presence as a precious and acceptable offering: thou hast prepared me for it, thou hast shown it to me, thou hast kept thy promise, God of faithfulness and truth. For this grace and for all things, I praise thee, I glorify thee through the eternal and heavenly high priest, Jesus Christ, thy beloved child: through Him, who is with thee and the Spirit, may glory be given to thee, now and in the ages to come. Amen.

Martyrum Polycarpi

---

8   Bouyer, 115.

Crisis

"Woe to you, scribes and Pharisees, you hypocrites.
You pay tithes of mint and dill and cumin, and have
neglected the weightier things of the law: **judgment** and
mercy and fidelity. [But] these you should have done,
without neglecting the others."

(Mt 23:23)

In the preceding words of Jesus from Matthew's Gospel,
we find the word *judgment* which is an English translation of
the Greek word κρισις (*crisis*). When we read these words of
Jesus we tend to think of judgment as the sorting out of the
faithful from the unfaithful—the sheep and goats in Matthew
25. In this passage the word *judgment*, translated from the
Greek *crisis,* pertains not to the final judgment but rather to
a judgment occurring in the here and now. The Pharisees, in
the here and now, were neglecting the weightier things of the
law. They were more concerned with rules than with persons,
with punishment than with mercy, with partiality rather than
equality and fairness. Jesus chastised them for their attitude
toward things that were less important while neglecting the
more important. Jesus was calling the Pharisees to a *decisive
moment*—their concerns would show either a desire for God or
against God by the way they were living.

We hear almost every day about some *crisis* that either
has occurred or is occurring. You may recall the *Ebola* crisis
which began in Western Africa or the pandemic crisis known
as COVID-19 which began in China. The COVID-19 virus
affected almost every part of our lives and resulted in people
working remotely from their homes, schools being shut down,

public Masses suspended, and so forth. We were made aware of an invisible evil whose contagion was in some cases deadly.

The educational system in the United States is in crisis, according to some experts. Along with state-mandated proficiency tests revealing a trend toward lower achievement scores, there is also the question of what type of education best serves our students. In addition to the education crisis based on curriculum and achievement scores as well as growing numbers of student illiteracy, another factor has surfaced. Parents and educators are increasingly concerned about the crisis with regard to student safety due to the increased number of school shootings.

The word *crisis* most commonly means some type of situation that is difficult or dangerous and which requires serious attention. However, at an earlier point in our history, the word *crisis* referred to the turning point for better or for worse in an acute disease or fever. Was Johnny going to make it or not through the night? That was the moment of crisis. It was a decisive moment.

Although we have an understanding of the word *crisis* in the English language, its original meaning comes from the Greek κρισις which refers to a *decisive moment which allows us to make a judgment*. As we consider the Eucharist and how the Real Presence of Christ is given to us in the sacrament of His Body and Blood, the decisive moment focuses upon faith. The decisive moment asks this question: How has Christ's light shined through me today?

For the Jews who wandered in the wilderness and who received the manna, it was a decisive moment for them to place their faith in God's Providence. Similarly, when Jesus fed the five thousand with only a few loaves of bread and fish, it was a decisive moment for them to believe in His power. In both cases, providing the manna and providing the bread, a miraculous event occurred. If those miracles could take place—and did take place—then were they not a prelude to the greatest miracle in which Jesus would take bread and wine and transform them into His sacramental presence? If the Eucharist is a greater miracle than the manna in the desert (see Jn 6:49-51) and greater than the multiplication of the loaves (see Jn 6:23-27), then how can the Eucharist be anything but the Real Presence of our Lord? This, however, remains the decisive moment for Christians. Some say they believe the Eucharist is *symbolic* rather than *real*. And so the κρισις exists for us today, just as it did for the disciples who either left Jesus or remained with Him when He spoke to them about the bread of eternal life.

****

When we hear the word *crisis*, our minds usually associate it with something that requires serious attention. A κρισις is a decisive moment. Receiving Our Lord in Holy Communion should always be done with serious attention, for it is one of the most decisive of moments in our life. When we receive Jesus we are saying that we will follow Him and turn away from whatever displeases Him.

I have come to realize with the passing of time that when I receive Holy Communion I am receiving Christ's peace, a peace that this world cannot give (see Jn 14:27). During the Mass, immediately preceding our reception of the Eucharist, we hear these words: *"Lord Jesus Christ, who said to your Apostles: Peace I leave you, my peace I give you, look not on our sins, but on the faith of your Church."* Following this prayer we are invited to offer to one another a sign of Christ's peace.

I believe that the peace of Christ, a peace that this world cannot give, is a peace that remains with us in order to help us persevere against the power of sin. The power of sin is real but the peace of Christ helps us to persevere in the *decisive moments* when we are tempted to sin. It is the peace of Christ that allows us to remain steadfast in the face of evil and it is the peace of Christ that offers us forgiveness when we succumb to evil. Again, if we consider the prayers that are offered immediately before receiving Our Lord in the Eucharist, we realize that the Lord's Prayer is among them. The Lord's Prayer concludes with *"but deliver us from evil,"* literally asking that we be delivered from the "evil one," the devil. Immediately after the Lord's Prayer we hear these words: *"Deliver us, Lord, we pray, from every evil, graciously grant peace in our days."* The Body and Blood of Christ, offered to us in the sacrament of Holy Communion, provide nourishment and strength. Christ's Body and Blood provide nourishment in faith and strength against the power of evil. When I receive the Lord in Holy Communion, I receive His Body and Blood and I receive the peace of Christ that this world cannot give.

When we offer to one another the sign of Christ's peace, it is far more than a greeting and wishing someone a good day. It is extending Christ's peace to remind us that we can persevere in doing Christ's work even in the midst of evil. In that way, offering to another person the Sign of Peace at Mass is also a decisive moment. The Sign of Peace is a way of saying, "Despite the power of evil all around us, may you have Christ's peace to guide you and to help you persevere." Following that, we ask the Lamb of God to have mercy on us and to grant us His peace. For this reason, I believe that when I receive Holy Communion I am receiving the Body and Blood of Christ Who offers me His peace—a peace that will be with me to help me in those *decisive moments* when the evil one tries to interrupt my life with temptations to sin.

****

Summary statement:

There are many decisive moments each day. What will I do next? How will I treat the person who has injured or ignored me? What should I make for dinner? Should I let the kids go out with their friends tonight or not? What book do I want to read? How will Christ's light shine through me today?

True, one may know man's final goal: communion with
God. And one may describe the path to it: faith, and
walking in the commandments, with the aid of divine
grace. One need only say in addition:
here is the path—start walking!

Saint Theophan the Recluse
The Path to Salvation: A Manual of Spiritual Transformation

Conclusion

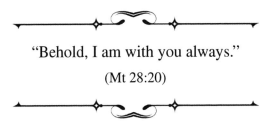

"Behold, I am with you always."

(Mt 28:20)

Phil, a gentleman of whom I had heard but had never met in person, died in the summer of 2017 when he was fifty years old. On the holy card that included his name and the dates of his birth and death, there was also a message that Phil had written, a portion of which stated the following: "There is a good way to die, and that is in the arms of Jesus. I pray that all of us use the time we have to become forever in His arms. It is easy to do; just ask Him to be with you always." Of course, Phil had it right because Jesus assured us that He would be with us always.

Jesus will be with us always—until the end of time and into eternity. In eternity we will experience immortality. The medicine of immortality, as stated so beautifully by Saint Ignatius of Antioch, is in the Eucharist.

The Medicine of Immortality

Most of us take some form of medication either daily or periodically. We take statins to lower cholesterol, cardiac medications for the heart, chemotherapy and radiation treatments for cancer, and pain relievers of all kinds. These are beneficial when used properly and can prolong life and better health. However, they are not the medicines of immortality.

From the Book of Numbers we find the story of the bronze serpent (see Nm 21:4-9). The king of Edom had denied permission to the Israelites to cross Edom on their way to Canaan (see Nm 20:14-21). Moses, therefore, rerouted the Israelites, making their journey longer and more arduous. In doing so "the peoples' patience was worn out by the journey; so the people complained against God and Moses" (21:4b-5). We then find in the story that venomous snakes bit many of the Israelites, who then died. The Israelites acknowledged their sin against God and asked Moses to intercede on their behalf: "Pray to the Lord to take the serpents from us" (21:7). The Lord then instructed Moses to take one of the serpents and mount it on a pole, "and everyone who has been bitten will look at it and recover" (21:8). Through God's providence a type of medicine was provided which allowed the Israelites to continue their exodus journey. What God provided was a supernatural remedy.

Focus your thoughts now to some 1400 years later. A Pharisee named Nicodemus came to Jesus one night, and Jesus instructed him on the necessity of a new birth that comes from God. At one point in the conversation Jesus said to Nicodemus, "And just as Moses lifted up the serpent in the desert, so must the Son of Man be lifted up, so that everyone who believes in him may have eternal life" (Jn 3:14-15). There are three other places in John's Gospel where we find mention of Jesus being lifted up (8:28; 12:32; 12:34) and each time it refers to Jesus' crucifixion. The Cross of Christ is the medicine that has redeemed us from sin. At each Mass the Cross of Christ is re-presented in an unbloody manner. At each Mass we are able, when properly disposed, to receive the crucified and risen Jesus Who comes to us in a moment of divine communion—Holy Communion. With this medicine, however, we are given the pledge of future glory. This is the medicine of immortality and becomes so when the priest, during the consecration of the Mass, lifts up the Sacred Host and the chalice that contains Jesus' Blood. It is, as Father Benedict Groeschel writes, "the life-giving and unmerited relationship of parental love with God to the whole being of the broken and bent human creature."[1]

---

1   Benedict J. Groeschel, C.F.R., *In the Presence of Our Lord: The History,*

The Tree of Life

In the second chapter of Genesis we read that God planted a garden in Eden and that in the middle of the garden was the tree of life, "delightful to look at and good for food" (Gen 2:8). We know the story—sin, suffering and death resulted from the disobedience of Adam and Eve. God banished them from the garden, "stationing the cherubim and the fiery revolving sword east of the garden of Eden, to guard the way to the tree of life" (Gen 3:24).

In the Book of Proverbs we find the tree of life identified with Wisdom (see Prv 3:18; 11:30; 13:12; 15:4). God, in His goodness, allows human beings the opportunity to pursue wisdom and in so doing, they can be restored to the life that had become unavailable in Gen 3:24. God furthered His goodness by giving us His Son, Jesus, the new Adam. On the cross we have a new tree of life, and the fruit of the tree is Jesus Himself. Furthermore, just as Adam and Eve had their eyes opened after sinning, the two disciples who encountered Jesus on the road to Emmaus had their eyes opened and they saw the fruit of our redemption. They saw the real presence of Christ who died and rose to redeem us from sin. Jesus, the new Adam, reversed the original curse that had been caused by sinful humanity.

In Jesus the tree of life is made accessible to all human beings (Rev 2:7; 22:2, 14). As such, the exclusion from the tree of life that occurred for humanity due to Adam's sin was revoked by Christ. Those who "wash their robes" in the blood of the Lamb will "have the right to the tree of life and enter the city (i.e., the heavenly Jerusalem) through its gates" (Rev 22:14).

The final verses from the Book of Revelation contain these words of Jesus:

> If anyone takes away from the words in this prophetic book, God will take away his share in the tree of life and in the holy city described in this book. The one who gives this testimony says, "Yes, I am coming soon." (Rv 2:19-20)

Theology, and Psychology of Eucharistic Devotion (Our Sunday Visitor: Huntington, IN, 1997), 18.

Christ promised that He will come soon. Until that occurs we have the assurance that Jesus is with us always (Mt 28:20). To that point, we say and believe that Jesus is present to us in the sacraments. In the sacraments we encounter the presence of Jesus who is with us always. Interestingly, many of the sacraments utilize the oils that are blessed each year at the Chrism Mass. The oil that is used for our sacraments is olive oil. The connection of the olive oil to the tree of life is found in a non-biblical Jewish text known as *The Life of Adam and Eve*.[2] The text indicates that the tree of life from the Garden of Eden was an olive tree. Where Adam and Eve were banished and could no longer eat from the tree of life, restoration would come through Jesus, the new Adam. Because of Jesus, we are offered the promise of eternal life that was originally the gift bestowed upon Adam and Eve until they sinned.

Our task is to grow in the life of virtue, especially in Christ-like love. The Eucharist allows us to partake of the risen and glorified Christ who remains with us always. Being united to Christ in the Eucharist offers to us the promise that we shall someday eat from the tree of life.

"Take and eat"

Jesus' words to His apostles at the Last Supper were to "take and eat." Eating is a theme that we find throughout Scripture. In the Genesis story Adam and Eve eat the fruit from the forbidden tree, and feeling their shame, they hid from the presence of God (see Gen 3:9-15). The original sin separated them from their original purpose of being united with God. Instead, because of sin, they had turned away from God's Divine Presence.

At the time of the Passover, the Israelites were commanded by Moses to eat the roasted lamb (see Ex 12:8-12). When we examine the details of the Last Supper we find that Jesus saw

---

2   An English translation of this text is by L.S.A. Wells from *The Apocrypha and Pseudepigrapha of the Old Testament in English, Volume II Pseudepigrapha*, edited by R.H. Charles, Clarendon Press, 1913.

Himself as the new Passover lamb. At the time of Moses the Exodus journey began after the killing of the lambs and the eating of their roasted flesh. So, too, the new Exodus would begin with eating the flesh of the Lamb of God whose blood would be shed for the forgiveness of sins. Just as eating was a part of the Exodus story, so, too, eating was important at the Last Supper.

During the wilderness sojourn the Israelites were instructed by Moses about the covenant that God was making with them. Following the covenant ratification, we read:

> Moses then went up [the mountain] with Aaron, Nadab, Abihu, and seventy elders of Israel, and they beheld the God of Israel. Under his feet there appeared to be sapphire tile work, as clear as the sky itself. Yet he did not lay a hand on these chosen Israelites. They saw God, and they ate and drank. (Ex 24:9-11)

In the Book of Revelation we are given a description of the new Heaven and the new Earth, where the thirsty will be given a "gift from the spring of life-giving water" (Rv 21:6). The life-giving water will flow "from the throne of God and of the Lamb" (Rv 22:1) and "On either side of the river grew the tree of life that produces fruit twelve times a year, once each month; the leaves of the trees serve as medicine for the nations" (Rv 22:2).

The first biblical account of eating resulted in sin. The final biblical account results in triumph over sin and its consequences. For us, the invitation remains to "take and eat." Blessed are those who partake of the medicine of immortality. Blessed are those who eat from the tree of life. Blessed are those who "take and eat" as Christ has commanded.

The Door, the Dining, the Divine

There is a beautiful image contained in the Book of Revelation which begins by telling us that the revelation comes from Jesus Christ and was given to John. We are also told that those who read or listen to the revelation will be blessed (Rev 1:1-3). The image is found in Chapter 3 from the Book of Revelation with these words of Jesus: "Behold, I stand at the door and knock. If anyone hears my voice and opens the door, I will enter his house and dine with him, and he with me" (Rev 3:20).

Jesus never forces us to accept His invitation. He never forces us to accept His love, nor does He force us to love Him. God has given us free will, and we can choose to either respond to Christ's invitation or to ignore it. The choice is ours. Nevertheless, Jesus tells us in this passage that He will continue to pursue us because of His desire to offer the promise of eternal life. He will continue to knock at the door of our hearts and our lives. If we choose to invite Jesus into our lives and open the door to Him, He says that He will dine with us. This is a beautiful Eucharistic theme that will conclude with the messianic banquet in heaven. Until the time of the heavenly banquet, we dine with the Lord most concretely in Eucharistic Communion.

This passage from the Book of Revelation echoes a parable found in the Gospel according to Luke. Jesus was dining at the home of a leading Pharisee and noticed how several of the guests scrambled for a seat of honor at the table (Lk 14:7). He then spoke about taking the lower place at table and being invited to a higher position, rather than taking the higher position and being embarrassed when asked to move lower. Jesus also stated that rather than simply inviting the wealthy and the prestigious to a banquet, it is better to also invite the poor and those with physical impediments. Jesus concluded His remarks by saying: "Blessed indeed will you be because of their inability to repay you. You will be repaid at the resurrection of the righteous" (Lk 14:14).

Immediately following this parable, one guest at table said, "Blessed is the one who will dine in the kingdom of God" (14:15). Dining in the kingdom of God is precisely what John addressed in the vision from Revelation 3:20. Jesus invites us to dine in God's kingdom and to rejoice in the heavenly banquet. However, the choice is ours. In Luke's Gospel, after the guest spoke about those who will dine in the kingdom of God, Jesus reiterates that while the invitation is given, we are free to accept or decline. In this regard, Jesus spoke about a great dinner to which many were invited. However, many excused themselves and declined the invitation.

One more occasion from Luke's Gospel when Jesus spoke about dining in the kingdom is found in Chapter 22. The setting was the Last Supper when Jesus celebrated the Passover with His disciples. Jesus had just indicated that He would be betrayed and the disciples were wondering who would do such a deed. But then an argument erupted when they questioned among themselves as to which of them was the greatest. You can almost imagine the exasperation within Jesus at that moment. He had just mentioned His upcoming betrayal, and the disciples started arguing about who was the greatest among them! Jesus reminded them that the greatest among them would be the one who serves the needs of others. He then said to them with regard to dining: "It is you who have stood by me in my trials; and I confer a kingdom on you, just as my Father has conferred one on me, that you may eat and drink at my table in my kingdom" (22:28-30).

Returning again to the passage from the Book of Revelation, Jesus calls us to be His disciples. Just as He reminded His disciples about service at the Last Supper, so He reminds us today about service. He told us that whenever we serve the least of His brothers and sisters, we do so for Him. Those who serve in this way will hear the invitation to "inherit the kingdom prepared from the foundation of the world" (Mt 25:34).

We have a divine invitation. We have a door to our hearts and our lives that we can choose to either open or not open to the Lord who stands knocking. If we open the door and accept what Jesus has asked us to do, we can also accept what Jesus offers—the opportunity to dine with Him. We dine with Him in a most profound way through Eucharistic Communion. This is the way that He has chosen to remain with us until the time of the messianic banquet.

In conclusion, we are nourished with the bread of Holy Communion so that we can receive God's divine life here and now. We are also nourished with the bread of Holy Communion so that we can receive eternal life in the hereafter.

Therefore, holy Father,
as we celebrate the memorial of Christ your son,
our Savior,
whom you led through his Passion and Death on the Cross
to the glory of the Resurrection,
and whom you have seated at your right hand,
we proclaim the work of your love until he comes again
and we offer you the Bread of life
and the Chalice of blessing.

Look with favor on the oblation of your Church,
in which we show forth
the paschal Sacrifice of Christ
that has been handed on to us,
and grant that, by the power of the Spirit of your love,
we may be counted now and until the day of eternity
among the members of your Son,
in whose Body and Blood we have communion.

Eucharistic Prayer V2:
God Guides His Church Along the Way of Salvation

The greatest love story of all time
is contained in a tiny white host.

Venerable Archbishop Fulton J. Sheen

Sources

Andersen, Frank, M.S.C. *Making the Eucharist Matter* (Ave Maria Press: Notre Dame, IN), 1998.

Beckman, Kathleen. *Rekindle Eucharistic Amazement: Healing and Holiness through the Mass and Holy Hour* (Queenship Publishing: Goleta, CA), 2008.

Bouyer, Louis. *Eucharist: Theology and Spirituality of the Eucharistic Prayer* (University of Notre Dame, Notre Dame, IN), 1968.

Burke, Raymond Cardinal. *Divine Love Made Flesh: The Holy Eucharist as the Sacrament of Charity* (Catholic Action for Faith and Family: San Diego, CA), 2012.

Clark, Stephen B. *Catholics and the Eucharist: A Scriptural Introduction* (Servant Publications: Ann Arbor, MI), 2000.

Dollen, Charles, ed. *The Holy Eucharist* (Alba House: New York), 1999.

Emminghaus, Johannes H. *The Eucharist: Essence, Form, Celebration* (Liturgical Press: Collegeville, MN), 1997.

Groeschel, Benedict J., C.F.R. *In the Presence of Our Lord: The History, Theology, and Psychology of Eucharistic Devotion* (Our Sunday Visitor: Huntington, IN), 1997.

Hahn, Scott. *The Lamb's Supper: The Mass as Heaven on Earth* (Image: New York), 1999.

Irwin, Kevin W. *Models of the Eucharist* (Paulist Press: New York/Mahwah, NJ), 2005.

La Femina, Anthony A. *Eucharist and Covenant in John's Last Supper Account* (New Hope Publications: New Hope, KY), 2012.

McGuckian, Michael, S.J. *The Holy Sacrifice of the Mass: A Search for an Acceptable Notion of Sacrifice* (Gracewing: Herefordshire, England), 2005.

O'Connor, James T. *The Hidden Manna: A Theology of the Eucharist* (Ignatius: San Francisco), 2005.

Pitre, Brant. *Jesus and the Jewish Roots of the Eucharist: Unlocking the Secrets of the Last Supper* (Doubleday: New York), 2011.

_____. *Jesus and the Last Supper* (Eerdmans: Michigan), 2015.

Rosetti, Stephen J., ed. *Born of the Eucharist: A Spirituality for Priests* (Ave Maria: Notre Dame, IN), 2009.

Schneider, Athanasius. *Dominus Est—It is the Lord!* (Newman House Press: Pine Beach, NJ), 2008.

Shea, Mark. *This is My Body: An Evangelical Discovers the Real Presence* (Christendom Press: Front Royal, VA), 1993.

Vorgrimler, Herbert. *Sacramental Theology* (Liturgical Press: Collegeville, MN), 1992.